The Shaman Speaks

How to use the Power of Shamanism
to Heal Your Life Now

By Shaman Elder Maggie Wahls

Real questions from real students
about life, living and power

Answers to the questions of living in this modern age
from a Traditional Indigenous Shaman

Foreword by Dr. Lori Lee

Modern Spirituality Series

Marvelous Spirit Press

The Shaman Speaks: How to use the Power of Shamanism to Heal Your Life Now
Copyright (c) 2011 by Maggie Wahls. All Rights Reserved.
from the Modern Spirituality Series
Cover picture from National Geographic. Reproduced with permission.

Library of Congress Cataloging-in-Publication Data

Wahls, Maggie (Jean Maggie), 1952-
  The Shaman speaks : how to use the power of Shamanism to heal your life now / by Maggie Wahls.
       p. cm. -- (Modern spirituality series)
  "Real questions from real students about life, living and power; answers to the questions of living in this modern age from a traditional indigenous Shaman."
  Includes bibliographical references and index.
  ISBN-13: 978-1-61599-007-8 (pbk. : alk. paper)
  ISBN-10: 1-61599-007-0 (pbk. : alk. paper)
  ISBN-13: 978-1-61599-063-4 (hardcover : alk. paper)
  ISBN-10: 1-61599-063-1 (hardcover : alk. paper)
  1. Shamanism. I. Title. II. Title: How to use the power of Shamanism to heal your life now. III. Series.

BF1621.W34 2010
201'.44--dc22
                                                    2010036709

Distributed by Ingram Book Group, New Leaf Distributing

Marvelous Spirit Press, an imprint of
Loving Healing Press
5145 Pontiac Trail
Ann Arbor, MI 48105

www.MarvelousSpirit.com
Tollfree 888-761-6268
FAX 734-663-6861

Table of Contents

Table of Contents i
Acknowledgments i
Foreword iii
Introduction v
Chapter 1 – Committing to the Path 1
  1. "Why study Shamanism?" 1
  2. "Where am I supposed to make room in my life to study any spiritual practice?" 3
  3. "Am I ready to become a healer?" 8
  4. "Is there any one to help me do this work?" 12
  5. "What is the most important quality to nurture?" 13
  6. "Does a person need an initiation to be a Shaman?" .. 16
  7. "Every time I try to walk my path as a healer something gets in the way. Why is that and what can I do about it?" 17
  8. "Is Meditation required in Shamanism?" 19

Chapter 2 – Energy Signatures 23
  9. "What is an energy signature?" 23
  10. "Does a crystal have its own energy?" 25
  11. "Are Spirit Guides the same as Totems?" 27
  12. "Do you hear voices?" 29
  13. "What of the earth's trembling?" 31
  14. "Why am I feeling more physical sensations in my body as I study energy signatures?" 33

Chapter 3 – Talismans and Tools of the Shaman 35
  15. "What is a power song and where do I get one?" ... 35
  16. "What is a medicine bag and how do I make mine?" 36
  17. "What is a Prayer Tree?" 39
  18. "Why are there so many different kinds of medicine wheels?" 40
  19. "What do animals tell us?" 43

20. "When you refer to the talismans (i.e. stones, feathers, etc.) being presented to us, do you mean on our inner journeys or in the physical world?".. 45
21. "What is a talking stick?" 46
22. "Do most people require physical symbols to accept that someone is able to perform a healing and to display that the healing act has been accomplished?" 46

Chapter 4 – Safety and Protection 49
23. "How do I stay safe in this reality and in others?" 49
24. "Can you give me a surefire way to be grounded and protected?" 49
25. "Should I fear studying Shamanism?" 51
26. "I have visions. Is that good?" 53
27. "How do you communicate with your guides and teachers?" 56

Chapter 5 – Traditional Shamanic Wisdom 61
28. "Can you explain what 'grace' is?" 61
Power. 65
29. "What is the deal with 'good versus bad'?" 67
30. "I realize I am human but I have a hard time when it comes to forgiveness." 68
31. "You frequently use the terms Causal and Buddhic. What are their meanings?" 73
32. "Is there a parallel between Buddhism and Shamanism?" ...77
33. "How does the Shaman define soul and spirit?.................. 80
34. "What good are emotions?" 82
35. "What does personal power have to do with Shamanism?" 86
36. "What do you mean by the word 'intent'?" 89

Chapter 6 – Standing in Your Power 93
37. "How would you say one develops personal power? I tend to have a very aggressive, controlling personality, which hinders me in many areas." 93
38. "I feel I am here to help heal the rifts in Mother Earth's energies. Can you tell me how to go about this?" 95
39. "How do I manage my time and balance myself in this hectic world?" 99
40. "Why do all these difficult experiences keep happening to me?" 100

41. "Do I control my emotions or do they control me?" 102
42. "I have the sensation of swimming or flying up to a different point in time. 103
43. "I have a hard time staying focused. Any suggestions?" 104
44. "What does a Shaman know that most people don't?" 105
45. "How do you protect yourself from predatory spirits?" 107

Bibliography 111
About The Author 113
About the cover 116
Index 117

The Modern Spirituality Series from Marvelous Spirit Press

The True Nature of Tarot: Your Path to Personal Empowerment by Diane Wing

The Shaman Speaks: How to use the Power of Shamanism In Your Own Life Now by Shaman Elder Maggie Wahls

Awakening Consciousness: A Woman's Guide! by Robin Marvel.

Acknowledgments

I would like to thank my good friend Maureen Rivelle for her many hours editing this book and for all her encouragement.

I would like to thank all my students for their continued support.

I would like to thank my Shaman Grandmother who taught me everything in this book.

I thank Creator for letting me be here. Aho.

Foreword

If "Effectiveness is the yardstick of ability," then Shaman Elder Maggie Wahls certainly measures up.

As a natural healer, I have experienced hundreds of seminars, workshops, books, classes and many styles of teaching, but none quite like Shaman Elder Maggie Wahls'. Her no-nonsense and practical approach to traditional Shamanism is refreshing, and most of all applicable to everyday life. She stands out among the hundreds of teachers I have met as one of the most knowledgeable and down to Earth practitioners of our time. Her commitment to guiding her students to a path of clarity and understanding is second to none.

She has helped me to stand in my circle, find balance, quiet my mind, and be in my own power. Through her guidance I am able to expand my awareness to a new and exciting level. Each day, in my own power, I walk closer to Source. Her impact on my life and natural health practice is immeasurable and, thanks to her, I experience new perceptions daily. In addition to new awareness, Shaman Wahls has helped me find ways to make my everyday life easier. What a gift!

Through her apprentice courses, intensives, speaking engagements, and now her book *The Shaman Speaks: How to Use the Power of Shamanism to Heal Your Life Now*, Shaman Wahls gives all of us Traditional Shamanic knowledge in modern vernacular. I encourage anyone interested in expanding his or her own awareness and healing to take advantage of her ancient wisdom and individualized teaching methods.

This is not new information for most. The majority of people reading this have walked the Shamanic path in a previous lifetime. Shaman Elder Maggie Wahls can help anyone to reconnect with the planes where we all once walked, and to do so safely and with purpose.

I found this book to be an enlightening and a pleasant read. The question and answer format is easy to understand and the questions mirrored my own curiosities. Whether a beginner on this path, desirous to know what Traditional Shamanism really is, or already a healer looking to expand one's awareness, this book is a "must-read".

Dr. Lori Lee, ND, CTN, author of
Modeling a Healthy Family: Mind, Body and Spirit
Director of Blue Rose Holistics
Ripley, West Virginia

Introduction

This book is not about Shamanism but about how you can live in your own power, as taught by a traditional Shaman. Over the years, thousands of people have asked Shaman Elder Maggie the hard questions of life. In an effort to bring you the truth as Shamans all over the world recognize it, she presents here some of the questions that her students have asked her over the years and her poignant, loving words of shamanic truth for them and for you.

These questions are from your neighbors, your friends; questions that we all ask at one time or another during the course of this adventure called life. It is an extremely rare privilege to be able to sit in the presence of a traditional Shaman and find answers for those issues that most concern you. Usually, one would have to travel thousands of miles and trek into remote areas to find just such an indigenous Shaman.

We are truly blessed to have Shaman Elder Maggie in our presence today as she has been given the mission to bring the knowledge of the traditional Shaman into the modern day world. This book is her gift to you. This book is will enable you to sit at the feet of a traditional indigenous Shaman, one who is a master, a mystic and a visionary, to ask your pressing questions and receive those answers which are unlikely to be found in any other way.

These questions were chosen from thousands of others as they most represent the knowledge and skills that anyone can use to bring happiness, love and prosperity into their lives. The exercises and visualizations are taken from her course called Shaman Apprenticeship 101. More information about her courses can be found on her website at www.shamanelder.com

It is with love and concern as a healer that this book has been written. Its motive is to give you knowledge and truth as the Shaman knows the truth. Shamanism is not some mystical, magical power given only to a few. It is in knowing the truths and living them that anyone can claim their power and become free. To the extent that you do this, the power of Shamanism can be yours. It is what you do that defines you.

1 Committing to the Path

1. "Why study Shamanism?"

This is probably the most commonly asked question today. And do you know why so many people ask it? Because we are brought up in a society that does not have Shamanism. Worse than that, we are brought up without community. In the old days, we were raised with a strong community around us. We lived together, played together, grew up together and sometimes even died together. We had elders, doctors, teachers and advisors right there for us, within our strong, close-knit community.

Part of the work of Shaman elders was to watch the children of the community to determine what each child's strength was. Those skills or gifts were encouraged as the child grew into whatever came naturally to him or her. It was the community, the elders, the teachers, and the parents who realized the blessings, and who were happy to help the child be what he or she was meant to be in life.

Today, we have no such possibility for ourselves or for our children. For the most part, we are raised to fit into a box; to learn what everyone else learns and to ignore or abandon anything that does not fit into society's preset patterns and ideas. It doesn't have to be this way! We have a choice. It is not too late to look inside and find those special gifts we were born with by studying Shamanism.

What are these gifts? Healing the spirit is the primary function of a Shaman.

Soul-retrieval is the gift by which the Shaman retrieves pieces of a person's lost soul. This is often accomplished by journeying to the spirit world and requesting assistance from the spirits, ancestors, and guides that dwell in other realities or worlds. These beings assist the Shaman in discovering what is wrong with the person. They often help the Shaman contend with the being now possessing those parts to win them back and return them to the patient. Examples of people displaying the classic symptoms of needing a soul retrieval would perhaps include those suffering from a mental illness, those abused as children, or those who sense that something is missing in their lives.

Soul restoration consists literally of the restoring of one's soul. This gift is used when a person is near death and his/her soul seeks to move on. This "death" could be the result of a psychic attack or an accident from which the body has recovered physically, but not spiritually.

Hands-on healing is most certainly a shamanic gift. This technique is still widely used today by Reiki practitioners, massage therapists, chiropractors and Shamans. Shamanistic hands-on healing involves the energy or spirit of the Shaman working with the energy or spirit of the patient.

Divination is the gift by which a Shaman can foretell the future, describe the illnesses of people and find their cures. Divination shows the Shaman the path the patient should walk to receive their healing. The most common Shamanic method in divination is journeying to the Otherworld to request information from the elders, guides and spirits who live there. It has been said that Genghis Khan used his Shamans in this way.

Herbal healing gives credence to the true belief that the Shaman is a medicine man or doctor. Herbal healing began with the beginning of the earth. Many of the hunting and gathering tribes had the ability to heal with plants indigenous to their areas. Today, this knowledge is fast disappearing as Shamans everywhere try to support the preservation of indigenous plant life and the lore surrounding them.

Dreamwork or dream interpretation is another Shamanic gift for healing. Shamans will listen to the dreamer relate an unusual or disturbing dream, and work with it until they feel a connection to it. They may then dream that dream themselves in a lucid way to find the message and resolve the conflict presenting itself.

Soul leading is the process in which the Shaman will help those who are crossing over to find the Light. The Shaman is very familiar with this Light and usually sees it in the upper right of his/her field of inner vision. Anthropologist Mircea Eliade says that a Shaman is a "Master of the Ecstatic." The Shaman masters the ecstatic journey because it is here that the power to do these healings can be found.

Each of us has one or more of these gifts buried somewhere inside our spirits. Can you imagine how beautiful this world would be if each of us studied and mastered the gifts we were given? Who would be left sick? Or poor?

2. "Where am I supposed to make room in my life to study any spiritual practice?"

Aho Shaman Elder Maggie,

I don't have time to take a course or a workshop. I have a very full life with work and kids plus my own outside activities. I don't even have enough time for me!

Aho Student!

And now you are taking this course. This course is like a river. I give you an inner tube and you climb in and begin going down this new river. You see things on the shore that look like you and your life, and you see other people there waving at you. These are your guides and teachers and they are glad to see you here! And you find fruit hanging off overhead branches as you glide by. You eat plums and peaches of insight and experience on your ride. Savor them. You are riding your own river and at the end of it, in lessons 10, 11 and 12, the river opens out onto a beautiful lake that you will call home. Now if you choose to, you can grab a branch and stop the ride or grab a rock and hang on or get out of the inner tube and stand on the bank. These are all your choices. But there is no need to do that. You are safe, you are seeing you and coming into your own power; the power of the river.

When you describe all that you do in your busy life, I see you standing on the bank watching things floating by in your river. You're saying "Yes, that is mine. That is mine." and "That is mine, yep, those right there are my own!" But you are not in the river! Your life is going by while you stand on the riverbank watching it go! This course invites you to get into the river within the safety of your inner tube; to actually be in the river, flowing along, observing you and learning your power, your skills and your abilities that are right there in the inner tube, right there in your mind and heart now.

You might discover that some of the things that you saw in your river while standing on the river's bank were just reflections of things that are on the riverbank, such as your activities and outside interests. You asked, "Where am I supposed to make room in my life to study any spiritual practice?" Think about it. All these things you see from the shore are experiences and people floating by in the river of you!

Let yourself flow in the river created by this course. Let yourself take what resonates within you and try the exercises. Don't sweat anything; be still, calm and relaxed.

You have an inner tube that you are floating on in the river. You are completely protected! From what? Protected from losing yourself in the hubbub of life, protected from not being yourself, protected from not being loved, protected from not being where you are meant to be in order to receive. Isn't that enough protection for you?

If you fight the current, you are missing out on your life! Your life is the river! Sure, we don't know what is around the next bend, but whatever is there is okay because we have our inner tube! You can trust yourself, your higher self, to get you through anything that comes. There may be a beautiful waterfall and rainbow around that bend but you will never be able to see it while standing on the bank watching your life pass by. It is your choice, of course. But I jumped in with both feet and I am still floating... and so will you. I have seen so many things... beautiful, wonderful sights, people, healings and adventures. You can too! It's about being true to yourself and following your own unique river. We only get the opportunity to do this once in this lifetime.

Most of us don't realize that we have an inner tube that keeps us intrinsically safe at all times. The Yaqui "Brujos" or Shamans have a different way of explaining what this inner tube is, but the meaning is the same. The Tibetans also teach it but in a different way. The truth is that you are safe! Even after you die, you are safe! When you were created, you were given this inner tube which is a connection to your higher self, to your own Spirit and to the Source. It is a safety cord that is always present and cannot be taken away. The worst you can do is to ignore it or push it away.

And that is what many people do. Sometimes it is our parents who take its presence away from us and hide it from us because they want to make us dependent upon them. So they only allow us grab onto whatever cord of protection or security they alone might offer us. And then we fear letting go of them. Subsequently, our schools and our churches do the same thing to us! They say "If you leave this church, you will let go of our safety cord and be drowned". Governments do this, our jobs do this and our spouses do this, too. They say, "I have the only security cord, the only safety net for you and if you leave, or don't do things the way I want, you will drown."

But really, we have always had our own security cord, our own inner tube. Other people have hidden it from us because we might not have been so willing to use their cord and therefore we may not have given them our power and obedience, if we'd known we had one of our own all along. But we do have this inner tube from lifetime to lifetime. Ask a little child if they are protected by anything and they will say yes, that they feel protected. That is if their parents haven't already removed this protection from their consciousness.

You might feel as though you are already in the river because you have been studying the water in the river. You've been putting things into the river such as little paper boats, and you've been watching them float around to and fro. You have deliberately been putting things in and taking things out of the river for a very long time. You have paid much attention to your river from the riverbank. You have filled it with activities and outside interests and taken out any stray sticks, like studying spiritual matters or working on your own fears, that come along in its flow. Did you know that you could get seasick by watching a river flow, even though you never get into it yourself?

And what if there was a huge waterfall around the next bend directly in the path of you and your inner tube? You are safe in your inner tube! And what if there were rapids? The inner tube would safely come out the other side, with you in it! And what if there was really rough water? Just hang on and ride through it as you know you are safe and will come out the other side. Yes, there are waterfalls, rapids and rough water in every person's life. And what if you die? Your inner tube will safely carry you right through that as well!

Most people think they are not protected; they don't know they have an inner tube to keep them safe. And when the waters get rough they scramble for the cords that others have given them, to their church, government or spouse, and expect help and protection through that cord. Unfortunately, they usually get nothing from these cords. Often those life cords of protection that outside sources offer us, in return for our allegiance, (and our power) are not real; they cannot protect us. They are strings at best or more likely, entirely made up. And how that hurts the person who trusted and believed that they were protected by their family, church, school, government, job or spouse, when they get into a waterfall situation and find out that the cord they were holding onto cannot protect them and that they are on their own!

But if people knew about their inner tube, they would not be afraid of anything. They would know that no matter what happens, they are safe and protected by this inner tube that is so real and so much bigger and better than anything man can offer. I wish I could teach this to the world.

It is possible to jump into the river and float along. And when things get tough, you can scramble to the shore and yell for those people who said they had cords to protect you. Unfortunately, they won't come. Sadly, you are left standing outside of your authentic life again; not going into your river and again watching your life pass by.

You only have so many days to go down this river of life. At the end of the river is a beautiful sea; that is your destination, your goal, your home, a place of peace, light and love. So many people never get there in this limited time called life. I want to reach that place. I want to accomplish what I came here to do, which can only be done by reaching the sea. I am not going to spend my time standing on the riverbank waiting for other people to rescue me when I know they can't, missing out on all the wonderful chances to do my work and to find my tools and gifts in the river.

The gifts are there for those floating in their inner tubes. Where is my happiness? Where is my joy? Where is my prosperity? Hanging from limbs over the river as gifts for those who are floating in their inner tubes. You can't reach them from the riverbanks. So many people are standing on the riverbanks just putting activities into the river like little toy boats and watching them float. They think that is enough. But they never get the gifts that are just around the bend.

Life is all about having enough faith to know that you are protected. Who gives you this inner tube? You do! Before you ever came here you gave this inner tube to you! Can you have faith in you? Do you know the "higher-self you" who is completely, entirely and totally at one with the Source?

3. "Am I ready to become a healer?"

As I read this email with care, I was looking at you going through many different life situations from above with the help of my guides and elders. The first thing I noticed was how similar your life experiences were to my own. I too have felt rejection, abuse, and blame, and I've even been at the point of choosing whether to live or die a long time ago. Yes, me too.

And do you know what? So have many others who are taking this course. One of my students asked me why we had to go through so much suffering to reach this point of choosing Shamanism. You may remember from my website that I even talk about this on my home page. But let me tell you in other words.

We come from previous lives as healers. We made an oath at some point in the past to be a healer for all eternity. In the olden days we were born into a Shamanic community. The elder Shaman would recognize us as healers when we were even babies and begin to help us re-member the ways. Today there are few Shamans. We are born into a community that rejects Shamanism. Yet somehow we must remember our ways. So, many of us get tossed and tumbled through many good and bad experiences until we do re-member our ways or find a Shaman to teach us. It is like learning Shamanism on the high seas of the North Atlantic instead of the calm Caribbean, for which this little boat was built. Nonetheless, you are on the right path now and you are remembering your ways as a healer.

I also asked myself what good all these extreme experiences did for me. Why did I have to go through enough stuff to fill 3 normal lifetimes, so much more than it seems that others ever encounter in their whole lives? And the answer that I found is that all those experiences enabled me to understand completely what you have gone through. I don't just sit here and read your words and say, "I am glad I didn't go through all that! Sorry, sweetheart, I feel for you." I went through all these same experiences so that I can sit here and say, "I have been there. I have done that." I know what it is and what it does to you. I honor you for still being here. I honor me for still being here. I respect you and admire your strength, your courage to do what you feel is right in your heart, and your wisdom to see what is going on your life.

A good teacher is one who teaches from experience. I don't want to be taught about the Vatican from someone who has never even been there. I can learn that much by myself. But if the teacher has visited the Vatican, then he knows what it feels like, he remembers it himself and can teach me the many things that I can't get out of books.

So the reason I experienced all those things in my life is to be able to teach you. I have practiced traditional indigenous Shamanism as taught to me through my own family lineage for over 50 years. I have lived it through many different experiences. I know the bad experiences and the good experiences and I will lead you in the gentlest way of learning that I can. We do not do hallucinogenic trips or use starvation, sleep deprivation, scare tactics or even mutilation as some cultures do. I also don't teach my native cultural Shamanism because they have plants in Russia that they use in ceremonies that we can't get here. What is the point of teaching you something you can't practice? Are we living in Russia, South America or Alaska? Then why learn the Shamanism that is practiced there?

The Shamanism I teach is able to be practiced by modern people from within cities, in daily life, without a community to support you as a Shaman. Is it ideal? No, of course not. The ideal would be to have a community, as we had in olden days, which respects you and supports you in exchange for your prayers and healing. But that is not going to happen here today. Being a Shaman is a solitary thing to do. Yet, within this course, you find community! You can make friendships that will last a lifetime!

The ideal would also be to have you come and live with me for 6 months or a year in which I can work with you moment-by-moment on a daily basis, really get to know you and do these exercises with you in person; a situation in which you could learn from watching me live my life and train in the ways just like in the olden days. I wish I could do that for you. But it would take a lot of time and money on your part to do that. And if we wait for Shamans to re-member themselves in this manner, Shamanism will be limited to a very select few.

The very select few Shamans who are offering to exclusively teach in this way intend to keep the teachings to a few elite. This actually causes a kind of hierarchy, the you-versus-me mindset which actually goes against Shamanism. Do you know what I mean? It's like the hierarchy of a middle-ages church. Those who teach in this way are in fact saying, "I am somehow better than you and so I will keep my knowledge out of your hands. You are somehow less than me because I know something that you don't and you can't have it." This is completely opposite from the purpose of Shamanism. A Shaman is a healer and is here to heal, to unite, and to embrace.

So there is a big problem with those Shamans who are saying that the only way to re-member your abilities is to spend lots of time and money learning one-on-one with a Shaman in his culture and community. These same Shamans are constantly angry with me for teaching Shamanism on the Internet. They think I have some sort of 'auto-responder' course without any interaction with my students, that I created a cookie-cutter course that pops out people who think they are Shamans. Of course they would say that!

It frightens them to think that there might be a way to heal, to embrace, and to unite; to help people re-member their Shamanic ways using this simple tool—the Internet.

You know now that this is not a cookie-cutter course. You know that I require lots of work from my students, and most importantly lots of communication. If you can't be here with me, at least communicate with me as much as you can. It is a big job and a difficult job to see you from here, to get to know you, to see where you are going (even with the help of my guides and your guides) so I can light the way for your path.

How can I do what other Shamans can only do in person? How can I teach what other Shamans insist can only be taught in person? You know, for some students, I can't. They cannot communicate with me for whatever reason. We can't seem to understand each other well enough to do the work by emails and Instant Messages. And that is OK. At least they have the basics and they can go and find that in-person Shaman to work with that they need to learn from.

But many, many people can learn Shamanism in this manner. They do the work, they communicate with me, and we understand each other. Both the student's and my own guides help us to make a place somewhere in the etheric plane where we can meet, communicate and understand each other. The place of teaching is provided, even if it is not of this world. And for this I am ever so grateful!

You and I can create this place if you are willing. It requires the drive to learn, to walk and to talk with this Shaman. You already have this drive. Then it requires meeting me halfway with communication, telling me about where you are on your path so I can find you there and walk with you along your path, showing you the way the Shaman walks.

We walk your path, not mine. But if you don't call out to me, then I can't find you and light the way. If you don't speak a language I understand or if you don't understand my language, we will have a problem. I think our backgrounds and life experiences prove that we do understand each other very well, indeed. I think we are all here to be healers and some of us will find walking the path of shamanism is the perfect way to heal others and ourselves. Yes, you are ready to become a healer.

4. "Is there any one to help me do this work?"

This seems to be today's message. Everyone is asking the same question today in unprecedented numbers! It gives me the opportunity to tell you something important.

Yes, the responsibility is of course yours. But you do not have to do it alone! You have Wolf, Raven, guides, elders and wise beings that love you and care for you, who are just waiting to help you! They have the answers and know how to do the things you want to do! Invite them into your life, sit by the campfire in your meditation with them and call on them for their guidance. Let go a little and let those who love you show you the way. These are, after all, parts of your own higher self.

Why rely on just your physical, emotional and mental bodies to make all your choices and do all your work? Why not look to your Causal or Buddhic self for guidance and try to operate more from there? Yes, this may be above your usual reality or your usual way of living. However, I'm here to tell you that there is so much ease in letting go a bit and relying on your higher self for the wisdom you already have. Your guides and elders will come and be with you anytime you call them. You can sit with them by your fire and talk to them. You can learn about yourself from them.

In conversations with my guides, they've asked me to tell them what I believe. After answering them to the best of my knowledge, they have responded at times, "No, that is not true," and have proceeded to tell me what I truly believe. It may seem harsh, but it was quite an effective way to realize what I truly believe. I work with my guides and elders all day, every day. I don't move without realizing my higher self in these guides and elders. I have found that by operating just from my three lower bodies, physical, emotional and mental, I make many mistakes, misjudge things, and wander around kind of lost and unsure of what I really want. It is crazy to do this when we have an Astral body, a Causal body and an Buddhic body to work from!

We should be striving to reach these higher bodies. One way to accomplish this is to work with your guides and teachers, to know your allies and to relax and know that you do not have to be alone. Just welcome them and they will be there for you. How many times have I gone to my guides and asked questions about what my students have written me, such as, "What should I say to my student about those fire balls she saw?" Do you think that I come up with answers to questions such as these on my own? I am not that clever! Even after 50 years of practice, my lower selves are weak and slow, and constantly struggling with each other for domination. But when I am in my Causal body, I can connect to Wisdom and Light, see with peace and joy, and know with conviction what I need to do to bring healing.

5. "What is the most important quality to nurture?"

Walking in gratitude is not a hard thing to do; yet it is the basis of a happy life and your own personal power. Native Americans give thanks to Mother Earth for everything they have. Christians give thanks before they eat. Shamans give thanks to the universe for all that they are.

When we walk in gratitude, we again find that sense of wonder in everything around us. We realize the bounty that we have in life. We appreciate the beauty we see. We hear the beautiful winds in the trees. We smell the flowers. We know how much is given to us that we didn't even have to work for. We walk with a sense of smallness against this gift, this experience of life.

Being grateful is as much a part of being mature as having wisdom or discernment. Gratitude teaches us to admire those around us, to lend a helping hand to those who need one. And who are we not to be grateful? Do we not see the blessings of the air we breathe? Do we not realize how fortunate we are to be walking this land? Just look around at all the places you could be.

Did you have a good idea today? Be grateful for that! Did you eat today? Be grateful! Is there a dollar in your wallet? Can you be grateful for that? When was the last time you looked into the heavens and said, "Thank you!"

Albert Einstein was one of the greatest thinkers in history. He was always aware of what could have been and expressed his thanks each day. Gandhi had nothing and yet was one of the most grateful men who ever lived. It isn't about who you are, what you have, or what station in life you have been blessed with. It is simply about being. To be is worthy of thanks.

Some people feel they have nothing to be thankful for. But did they have air to breathe? Did they get up this morning and find the sun shining? Did they find another human being to talk to? Companionship, caring, compassion, beauty, life, seasons, the earth- these are all worthy of our thanks.

The Shaman cannot heal without gratitude. It is not the Shaman who creates any healing, who finds the lost souls, and who comforts the dying with hope in new life. These things are greater than any man, priest or Shaman. It is our interconnectedness with each other through the Creator that gives us what we need, what we want and even more than we can imagine.

Start each day with a prayer of thanksgiving. Tell the universe how happy you are to find the sun shining in your window, to hear the birds singing and see the green grass glowing with dew. Thank your Creator for the gifts you will receive this day. Humble yourself at the magnificent creation of life and give gratitude for being an observer of this most holy miracle today.

By giving thanks, you are opening yourself to all the possibilities of goodness. You are joining into the universal awareness as a participant in life. You are forming a council and taking your seat in the creation of the day. You come with open hands to receive and you are ready to give your blessings to those around you. You realize your fortune and you wish that same fortune for all.

Being grateful sets the tone for goodness and open communication with your teachers and guides. It shows your willingness to learn and your respect for what is. Gratitude manifests more things to be grateful for. If you make a list each day of those things you feel grateful for, you will find that your list will grow over time. It will change from things seen to those things that are unseen and far more important than material possessions or fame. You will touch the very fabric of your soul and feel the blessings you have that are so worthy of your gratitude. Gratitude begets humility in this awesome life experience. And in humility you will receive more than you could ever receive with pride.

A Shaman knows this humility and often falls to his knees to return the heartfelt love that he recognizes and honors. The power of the Shaman comes not from within but from without. A man standing on his own is just a man, but a man standing on the grace of gratitude walks with Spirit and is given everything – even the ability to heal. Approach each day, each hour, each minute with gratitude in your heart and find love filling your spirit with its own power and truth.

6. "Does a person need an initiation to be a Shaman?"

You ask if you have had an initiation. What I have found with most of my students is that they have already been initiated in a previous lifetime. They are already Shamans. Becoming a Shaman in any lifetime is a pact, a promise and a contract that exists beyond time and space. Once a Shaman, always a Shaman. You do not need an initiation because you already had an initiation, maybe thousands of years ago. Some of my students get to the end of the course thinking I will do some kind of initiation for them and give them some Indian name or something. Not so. They have been Shamans for a long time already. And if they have not, or came here just out of curiosity, they will not become Shamans just by reading this course.

They will have to practice and learn the skills and do the exercises over and over until Spirit feels that they are ready. Then they will have an initiation by Spirit, not by me. I am here to hold a torch for you to walk your path. I will remind you of the old ways and everything will seem strangely familiar. Your spirit guides, totems and helpers will come to you now and teach you what you have forgotten. They have prepared this course for you and asked me to walk with you and hold the torch. They will teach you. They are the ones who have told me what to write.

I will also tell you that you must practice, practice, practice. You are very rusty with your skills. The exercises in this course are for practice, not just one or twice but continually until you get all the meaning and all the experience that lies beneath their surface. As you do them over and over, you will find other things hidden inside them that I did not talk about. Like a hunter, you must get so good with your bow and arrow that you are the best hunter in the forest. How can you feed the village if you are not the best? This is where most of my students fall apart. They do not want to do the work.

How will they feel when this life is over and they are again between worlds looking at this life from above- seeing the reason they chose to come here now was to be a Shaman as they had contracted to do, and then seeing that they were too lazy to accomplish the purpose of this life? I would be so ashamed of myself! That would be like a hell to me to see that it was my own laziness and my own lack of ambition that made me fail at what I came here purposely to accomplish! I won't let that happen to me. I won't let that happen because it would hurt me so much to know that I had caused myself to fail. It would hurt me to see all the good I could have done on this earth, that I didn't get done because I was too lazy to practice, practice, practice. Again, I say that there are many layers to these lessons. You must do them over and over to peel off the layers and find the deeper teachings.

7. "Every time I try to walk my path as a healer something gets in the way. Why is that and what can I do about it?"

Sometimes we get "tested". We get asked by Spirit to make a choice. We find ourselves in a very uncomfortable place that we do not like and we have to make some sort of choice. Often we do not even know what the choices are! But I have learned that when you commit yourself to a certain path, every now and then along the way you will meet a path crossing yours, a detour, a sidetrack, or a u-turn. We all reach these places. If you are not committed fully to your path, then you will run into conflict when you encounter these places. You will start to feel unwell, dragged down, unsure, restless, and unhappy because you are being asked to once again confirm your commitment. You may have already found your path as a healer. You understand the power and the holiness of this path. And you may have already met a crossroads where you faltered and hesitated. You then reaffirmed your path as a healer once again and continued practicing; the crossroads was over and you continued to walk stronger than before!

It is only painful when we hesitate, when we are not sure about what we believe. Your own questioning of your healing path caused this presentation of a crossroads. We actually place these u-turns in front of our own selves. So by believing strongly in whatever you believe and being committed to whatever you believe, you will not see too many u-turns or sidetracks in your life. And when you do see them, you will recognize them as sidetracks and u-turns and just ignore them, or better yet, realize that you are trying to fool yourself. How do we fool ourselves? We say we do not have time for our healing gifts. We say they don't really work. We say we can't do it. We say we are too lazy to do it. But the truth is that your healing gifts do work, and you know it. Everyone has healing gifts and skills. You do have time for your healing path every day, all day long. It does not interfere with time for other things. You will have to judge yourself to see if other reasons have come up and if they are true or not. It is all about being true to yourself, being authentic.

Let's look at detours along the way. Somebody taught us how to put detours into our lives. They don't have to happen but they do, for nearly everyone. Somebody told us there would be snags in our lives. I say, "That's their belief, not mine". Somebody said into every life a little rain must fall. I say, "That's their belief, not mine". My Creator tells me that there is neither snag nor rain, only blessings, gifts, abundance, love, peace and joy. Anything else is the belief of others. Does it take determination to be a healer? Very much so! It takes commitment and determination to do anything worthwhile. In fact, the Yaqui Shamans say that a Shaman even needs to be *ruthless* in his or her pursuit of the Shamanic path. But when you weigh your efforts against the blessings that will happen through your efforts, the determination and striving for impeccability are a low cost for health, joy and abundance.

Committing to the Path

An old Yaqui Indian teacher of mine of long ago once told me an old saying of his people. It was that by the time you have finally learned what your path is and how to walk it, your legs are too old to do the walking! Do not let this happen to you. We need your healing and your light in this world *yesterday*! You can see all the healing that needs to be done here. You can see the people suffering, crying out, and lost in their own pathless lives. Today, you can do something about that. Today, you can live an impeccable life. You can do your very best in every way today, and that includes learning what you need to learn, practicing your skills and offering healing to those who come your way.

There is another truth given to me by this same teacher. He was a great teacher! He said that if you do not live your truth, then you are nothing. He taught me the meaning of truth not only in what I say, but in what I do and in how I interact with you as a colleague, a friend and a teacher. A person without truth is totally worthless. You cannot trust them, you cannot believe them, and you cannot depend on them to help you. And what do they have if they do not have their truth? Nothing. That is why I begin and end everything I say or write with the Yaqui word, "Aho!" which means in the Yaqui language, "I speak my truth."

My truth may be all I have to give you but it is my truth. I keep a sacred vow to myself to be in my truth at all times. In this, I have dignity, light and power. It is part not only of being a Shaman, but of being an authentic human.

8. "Is Meditation required in Shamanism?"

What a great question! As we all know, the Eastern religions suggest years of meditation to reach one's own intrinsic power. But what is the purpose of meditation for them? It is a way to center oneself. It is a way to put aside all the nonessential chatter going on in our minds every minute of our waking day. It is a way to detach from the here and now to find the eternal, the universal. It is a way to find your higher self, the person sitting in the control booth of your life, looking down and watching over you, which is also you. It is a way to connect to the Divine Consciousness, the Universal Oneness, whatever you would care to call this, and discover your Oneness. When you are in touch with this Oneness, this is when you best feel the power, your power, which is your ability to love, share and heal.

In Shamanism we try to be hunters and warriors. And what is the hunter doing while stalking his prey? Is he listening to the chatter in his mind? He is still and silent. He is completely aware, completely present in the here and now. He is attuned with nature both visible and invisible. He is in touch with the Universal Oneness through his impeccable training and intention to be fully aware and detached.

A hunter knows that as he hunts, so he is hunted. There are many things in the wild that would like to eat him. He must be on guard and be watching everywhere for danger. A hunter knows, in fact, that at any minute a lion or bear could leap out of nowhere and devour him. Isn't life this way as well? Are we not all in some peril of car accidents, fire or other dangers inherent in living? So the hunter lives his life in that knowledge, realizing that this might be his last day, his last hour. He lives it fully, in full awareness of the present moment, the now, and relishes it to the utmost. He takes excitement from each moment of the hunt and he hunts as though it is his last hunt, with all the attention, fervor and excellence of skill that he has.

We should live our lives in the same way. If we were to live in this way, we would be truly rich, our lives would be truly exciting and we would laugh with glee over even the smallest of treasures. It is called living impeccably.

So a Shaman does spend time in meditation, although he or she may not cross their legs and sit on the floor. A good Shaman sits in a meditative stance in the hunting blind, waiting, listening, and watching for the prey to arrive. It is a matter of survival for him to be able to sit in meditative awareness with arrow knocked and bow string taut. It is a good way to live. It is, in fact, delightful! It is called owning your own power. It is being in control of your self.

2   Energy Signatures

9. "What is an energy signature?"

Everything is energy. All energy has a frequency and a vibration that can be sensed. So we need to study the vibrations of each energy and identify it for what it is. One way to do this is to begin by sensing its energy vibration and then asking to see its three faces or by going backwards from its three faces to its energy signature. But it is this signature, which we can use to identify the spirit of something.

An example is fear. When we feel fear, we feel its vibration in the pit of our stomach or in the clenching of our throat. We all know what fear feels like. We know the energy signature of fear. It may look like falling from a high building, or a car coming too fast into a crowd of people, or getting swept up in a raging river. It has many, many faces but its signature is the same. So when we feel that feeling of fear, we look around to see how it is appearing at that time. Or maybe when we see one of the faces of fear, we feel its vibration in our stomachs. This is a very plain and basic example. The important fact is that everything has an energy signature.

The Shaman studies these signatures. He knows that the faces will change. He doesn't rely on the faces to recognize where that energy is derived from. And so when a crow comes to my house, I sense its energy signature. It may be my grandmother coming to tell me I should not drive on this day. Or it may be some other kind of message I can understand by its energy signature. So there are two parts. One is the bringer of the message and the other is the vibration of the message. But I don't want to get too far ahead here. An energy signature is a specific vibrating energy of spirit or soul composition along with the magnetic and gravitational aspects from all ten dimensions combined into a unique frequency specific to that being.

When the Shaman travels the Inner Worlds for a healing, he is often looking for a particular being that has had dealings with the client in question. How do I find the correct being? By looking for that being's or person's energy signature. How did I learn the signature? The client showed me the energy signature by thinking about that being or person himself.

When I do a soul retrieval because a being has taken power from a client, I just have to look for that power. The vibration of the client's power is the same as the client's energy. The signature is the same. I don't care what the being looks like. He has too many faces to care about. But I will know it is the being I am looking for. In this regard, Holographic Theory fits perfectly into Shamanism. It says that every small piece of a hologram contains all the pieces of the hologram.

Some of my students make their first journeys with me in the Practice 201 course to the Upper worlds to meet an Ascended Master or angel of their choice. How do they find this Ascended Master? First, they do a study about him or her. They do research, read and learn about this ascended soul. Why? So that they can recognize his or her energy signature. When your friend calls you on the phone, you recognize his or her voice easily. You don't have to ask who is calling. It is the same sort of thing. And if you think about it, when you think of Ascended Masters and angels, you can almost sense the energy signature of this kind of being already, can't you? There is a holiness, a sacredness and a general signature of enlightenment that we all can recognize already.

In your studies of energy signatures you will find that there are broad signatures, such as that of trees, which all have similar signatures. Yet the signature of a Yew is slightly different than that of an Oak. All animal life has a common general vibration but it breaks down into finer vibrations depending on the kind of animal. All people have a similar general signature, yet we each have a unique frequency. When you think of the psychic who can tell you that your deceased grandmother is here with you, how does he know it is not your Uncle Frank? By the energy signature. And how did he know your grandmother's signature? Because you know it! He can tune into you and find that signature. He can work with energy signatures. And so can you! All Shamans do. It just takes practice, awareness and discernment.

How do you know your totem is around you? By recognizing its energy signature. And what if your totem was a wolf but it showed up as a goose? Would you know the difference? The appearance may be deceiving but the signature never changes. So make it a game, a study, and learn to understand signatures and realize what great tools these signatures are for healing. All of my students have seen me. I show up in a dream or in their meditations or astral journeys. But do I look the same to everyone who sees me? Not at all! Yet it is me!

10. "Does a crystal have its own energy?"

Does a crystal have its own "self" outside of the spiritual connection you seek from it?

Unknown to many, a crystal has its own self outside of the spiritual connection you ask it for. Yes, a crystal has its own unique vibration and its own energy signature. Even the vibration of a ruby is different from that of a piece of quartz. Yes, a crystal is a manifested bit of Spirit.

My Shamanic training says that if your totem, for example a bobcat, wants you to have a stone to represent him, he will present you with that stone. You may find it on a walk or in a store but it will call out to you with the spirit of the bobcat. Do I think that you can ask or make bobcat put his energy into your stone for you? No, this would be a useless endeavor. It is up to Bobcat to give you this gift. It is not up to you to do some sort of ceremony to make it happen. Shamans work within the Universal Laws of Nature.

Actually a stone will come to you for many reasons. It may come to you to show you something you have overcome. For example, if you learn a lesson successfully, you may be given a stone to remind you of that success. It gives its energy for this purpose. Or a stone may be given to you to help you overcome some difficulty you are now facing, to give you strength, to give its energy for this purpose. Or a stone may bring healing to you or someone else. It gives its energy for this purpose. And these stones come to us. We accept their gifts to us. I know this seems to go against what many crystal healers teach but it doesn't contradict them in actuality. This way of understanding respects the inherent energy of each stone. And by respecting the energy of the stone and working with it, instead of trying to make it work according to your intention, you can get much farther ahead. Doesn't this make sense?

Take the time to recognize the energy of a quartz crystal. Get good enough at it that if someone had their hands behind their back and were holding a quartz crystal in one hand and a banana in the other, you would pick the hand with the quartz crystal. Go even farther so that you know the energy signature of a banana and then you can tell the person, "You have a quartz crystal in your right hand and a banana in your left hand." How do you do this? Take the time and do the work to study energy signatures.

It's just like learning to read books. By repeated exposure to the word "run", you learned to recognize it! Same thing! How can anyone expect to recognize the energy around them when they do not learn first how to read? That's like holding up the word "run" in front of a two year old child and asking him what it is. He may say it's a word but he would not know what word. You can sense energy, but you may not know what kind of energy it is. Start with things you know well, easy "words" like banana, car and cat. Learn their energy signatures. Later you can learn to differentiate between a Lexus and a Dodge, and between a Cheshire and a Lynx. Everything has an energy signature.

By studying energy signatures as if you were studying archeology at an ancient ruin, taking your time and being precise and patient, you can eventually recognize what is visiting you. One of the first things we begin to recognize about energy signatures is the basic good feeling or bad feeling we get from that signature. Using your emotions to help recognize energy signatures certainly is part of that way we do this. We use our emotional feelings, our mental acuity, our physical senses like shaking or coldness, our inner eyes, ears and feelings and also our astral selves to look at this energy from the astral place as well as our causal selves (when you have developed a working understanding of your causal self) to recognize these energies. When you get them all well developed and operating optimally, you will be able to recognize more and more "words", that is, energy signatures.

Everybody wants to jump right to the end of the book. We walk a path. Enjoy the path of learning this skill. It really is fascinating and a great walk to take!

11. "Are Spirit Guides the same as Totems?"

Spirit guides are not totem animals. A spirit guide is a teacher with something to teach you. A totem animal is a message bringer who shows you through is own skills and abilities what skills you need to incorporate more fully into your own life. Just look at that attributes of that totem.

For example, what if your totem animal was an elephant? If you look up the attributes of the elephant, you will see its characteristics are royalty, strength, ancient wisdom, patience, carefulness, confidence, and education. These would be the skills it is trying to show you that you need to work on within yourself. And when you have honed your own abilities in those characteristics you may find that totem animal leaves and another one takes its place.

Your totems choose you, as you are aware. It is an animal you have a special affinity for or have seen frequently and recently. Your totem animals will change during your life. As you grow and change, your totem animals may change as well. You may have several totem animals at once. But one is a life totem and represents your basic self or personality, your essence.

Spirit guides are teachers. They come to guide you in your education. They teach you things. They may have lived other lives. They may be "ascended" beings. Here is a nugget of wisdom: everything has three emanations, faces or appearances. We do, plants do, animals do and everything does.

When I go into the Inner Worlds to seek a healing for someone, I encounter some sort of being there who is responsible for the sickness. The first face it shows me is really goofy, odd or weird, and I know that this face is not representative of what it really is. So I ignore that face and ask to see its true face. The next face it shows, if it is not a nice being, is that of a ferocious, grizzly, nasty, or scary being who tries to bite me or otherwise scare me. But I am not scared because I know that this is not its true face, either. I may have to fend it off, deflect it, or protect myself from it but I am not scared of it. I ignore this second face and ask to see its true face for the third time. The third time I see what it really is. If it is not a nice being, it usually looks weak, small and very lacking in every department. This is the being I negotiate with.

So I know that everything has three faces. Another example is when I sit with a rock and it turns into a lily and then it becomes a butterfly and flies away. Or when I sit with a river and it becomes a meadow and then it changes into a bear walking away.

Can we have more than three faces? Yes! Some people have hundreds of faces. But everything has at least three. And usually the three represent a plant, an animal and a sky creature.

Your spirit guides will help teach you intent, emotional control, knowledge and impeccability, if you allow them. Remember, it is always your free will choice whether to learn or not to learn. But don't travel to the Inner Worlds if you have not mastered the skills necessary to be safe there and to do your work there. And never go there just out of curiosity. There are too many discarnate beings waiting for you to arrive there unaware, so they can get whatever they can from you. They can be tricky and sly, and even devious. Even one bee is enough to stay away from. It doesn't take a pack of grizzly bears to kill you.

12. "Do you hear voices?"

Yes, I hear my mother and father who have both passed over whispering in my ear, or sometimes as very loud, audible voices. I hear my guides audibly. Sometimes though, it feels like you are talking to yourself, but you realize that what is being said is not something you would say. Or sometimes I hear a whisper from the heart. You just know what you heard in your heart is from your guides. For me, it is a combination of all these things.

To hear, you only need to intend to hear. Then listen expectantly. Clear your own mumbling away and listen. Within just a few moments you will hear from outside yourself.

I also can see my mother and receive hugs and kisses from my mom and dad! I can hug them and they can hug me. Sometimes they hug me when I am not expecting it and I burst into tears of love in the middle of the sidewalk. I look like I just won the Miss America contest…I am so lit up with love and joy when that happens! In some Christian circles, this phenomenon is called being "Slain in the Spirit". It's when you feel that kind of love pouring into you from God and you feel as though God is right there hugging you and telling how much He loves you.

Many people begin to cry at the awesomeness of that realization; some people pass out or fall to the ground. For me, the love of my mother or father is exactly the same as the love of God. There is no difference. It is the same love. So does my mother represent God to me? Or does God represent your dad to you? It makes no difference. We are all One in Creator. That is why we *can* hear, see and get hugged by our loved ones who have passed. And you can take that across time into other lives and into other places to be hugged by Djwhal Khul or Archangel Ariel or even me! Find that connection and you will find an endless well of love to draw upon.

In my learning I have been taught and I believe that reincarnation does not occur very quickly. Our parents and loved ones who have passed over want to maintain a connection with us as we live out our lives, and so they do. They can reincarnate if and when they choose, and it's usually not until this generation and possibly the next has also passed over. We do not lose our connections with our loved ones. Our parents want to watch over us and be with us here and now. If you think about your own past lives, you will see a space of 50 years or more between them. The last time I lived here was about 1914. I lived in California and can take you to the place I lived out my last years. I can also show you where I lived in Ireland in the 1400s. Okay, it's getting way too spooky for you now, eh? It doesn't matter anyway. These are just historical facts. What matters is that we grow with each lifetime. We must re-member who we are and why we are here. We must find our own abilities for healing and use them to the best of our abilities. We must re-member our mission here to heal, teach or make a difference in whatever way we agreed to accomplish that goal.

13. "What of the earth's trembling?"

Dear Shaman Elder Maggie,
Thank you! I knew if someone could talk about what I was experiencing, it would be you. To me, it feels like the world is under a great deal of stress; there's a lot of tension on different levels: emotional and physical. It feels that, though it eases up, it's going to burst soon. For years I assumed (I don't know why) that when the tension is too great, and it pops, that this world, and another world (governed more by the mental and spiritual aspects than this one which is more physical and emotional) will be joined once more.

To my understanding that I've developed over the years, the world's tension is also like the spiral. It can relieve tension without bursting, but when it relieves it, it can only relieve so much; it eventually builds up to where it has to pop, and eventually an end comes. After that bursting has completed its purpose of relieving the spiritual, physical, emotional, and mental tension completely, then it continues up the spiral. But that's just the understanding of a novice. Thank you!

Aho, Student!
I know exactly what you mean about the stress on the planet. Many people have written about this and even those involved in Ascension who channel Masters such as Djwahl Khul and Metatron have spoken at length on this subject. I too have thought that some cataclysmic event might happen from the stress that is being manifested right now, but I was shown a vision of childbirth. When the mother is suffering those pains and stretching to birth her child, she does not explode but a new being issues forth from her own body.

When a volcano erupts, it shakes the ground and causes tremendous pressure inside the earth, until finally it issues forth heat, gas, lava and stone. What the masters are saying is that this stress on the planet will not cause it to explode, but will issue forth a new manifestation. I think that manifestation will be to a higher spot on the spiral.

People are becoming more aware of their spirituality today and are looking for answers, not just in the physical but also in spiritual realms. This is good. I think what will manifest will not be physical but will be spiritual, a new way of communicating and living in a spiritual way. So my take on the stress that we are seeing is that it is a good thing and will bring us new light and understanding, compassion and cooperation on a spiritual level. Even the Bible talks about the end times as having a period of peace and cooperation. But right now, as we go through this period of unrest, stress and upheaval, it is up to us each individually to try our best to understand the spiritual side of life so that we can help those who are behind us when we reach that period of peace.

I read a wonderful article saying that healers today are standing at the far end of the rainbow bridge to Spirit and trying to teach from that point. But most people today are standing at the near end of the bridge without knowledge or understanding and they don't even see the healers on the other side. So it is important for us who have some knowledge and who want to teach, to go over to the near side of the bridge where the majority of people live and work and to teach from that place, to welcome them onto the bridge of spiritual enlightenment. The article also said that this is the reason why healers are not making a living today teaching; they are too far removed from their students.

My aim as a Shaman is to stand on the near side of the bridge and give a lighted torch to show the way across the bridge for anyone who is willing to learn. Work with your friends and family and your coworkers; make yourself available to answer questions. Let them know that you have some answers, if they want to know. Stand up and be counted for the powerful healer you are. No one will shoot your head off! Be a beacon wherever you go.

We are here to help this new birth. We have been chosen because we are willing to learn, study, practice and improve, and we are strong enough to withstand the trembling of the birth pangs. I hope I have shed some further light on this truth for you! I honor and respect you for being willing to listen and I hope you will be able to speak to those who ask!

14. "Why am I feeling more physical sensations in my body as I study energy signatures?"

You are becoming more aware of the energies around you. You are letting the Novocain wear off after the dental visit. This is a great question and one that I wish people asked more often. You have chosen to allow yourself to feel the energies of more things; many more things. How can you learn energy signatures if you are not open to sensing them? And as you open up to sensing them, you are indeed sensing them. And you sense them, as I said above, with all your senses, both physical and spiritual. Some psychics only use physical sensations to determine the identity of an energy. Well that is a handicap!

Imagine a psychic explaining before a reading, "I can tell the energy that makes me shiver when it is around me, the energy that gives me goose bumps and the energy that makes my heart leap. I can recognize three energies. I am psychic! Let me do your reading based on these three physical sensations!" I don't think most people would have confidence in this psychic's abilities to give an accurate reading!

Use all your senses. They tell you things. There is nothing scary about goose bumps or heart leaps. They are sensors! We are sensory beings! Learn about your sensors and learn how to pay attention to them, what they mean and how to use them. Don't give me a Geiger counter without any directions and then put me in a padded cell! Let's take this great machine outside, figure out how it works and go find things that make it go "Beep, beep, beep!" Let's work with this machine and get good at it!

3   Talismans and Tools of the Shaman

15. "What is a power song and where do I get one?"

Power Songs are oral prayers expressing your true self, your nature, your individuality, and your power. All cultures have power songs and you can have your own power song, too. We think of the power in a hymn or an African chant, in a Shamanic ceremony song or even in the howling of a wolf. There is a definitive power in sound.

All Shamans have a power song. The vibration of the notes in the voice and in the fourth chakra of the throat stimulates sympathetic vibrations in the universe to respond. Everything is connected. What you put out comes back to you. When a butterfly flutters his wings in Cost Rica, the winds of Africa are stirred. And when a sound is offered, the universe responds.

Power songs are used in preparation for journeying, healing, offering Reiki, praying, and grounding. They are used for protection, for celebration, for solace, and actually for any time you want to connect with the universe in this very special way. To demonstrate the power of voice and musical notes, I would like to you try this exercise:

The fourth chakra is the fourth note FA as in Do Re Me FA. Find a piano or another musical instrument to learn the sound of the note F above Middle C, if possible. Or ask someone to play this note for you on any tuned instrument. It is important to find the actual sound of FA.

The fourth note F or sound of FA is also the note of manifestation or creation upon this planet. So if we want to manifest healing, for example, we can send our intention out upon the note FA into the universe, and healing will resonate with our intoning of the note FA to become manifest where we are intending. It really is that simple.

Don't try to complicate it as so many others have. This simple little secret is one for which some people have paid thousands of dollars. Some people have made millions creating musical CDs based on the sound of FA. Many subliminal recordings, new age music or holosync CDs that offer healing or increased creativity, or that are meant to help you manifest abundance, are based upon the sound FA. But now you know how to do it yourself. And Shamans have been using sound for healing for tens of thousands of years.

If you wish to look at it visually, the square is the symbol of 'creating' in the universe. The square represents vibrations of the universal energy becoming manifest on the physical plane. So let's combine the sound of FA with the visualization of a square.

Find yourself a comfortable place where you will not be disturbed for a while. Close your eyes and visualize a square. Intone the sound FA and watch the square to see what image appears there. Let me know what you see.

16. "What is a medicine bag and how do I make mine?"

A medicine bag is an ancient item that spiritually represents the person who wears it. In 1991 the body of a man who lived over 5,000 years ago was found frozen in a high mountain range. With him was a medicine bag. The medicine bag is known in all cultures and is seen throughout all of history.

The Shaman often carries a medicine bag that has items in it for healing oneself and others. Other reasons to carry one are for guidance and protection. It may contain objects such as leaves, feathers, stones, herbs such as sweetgrass, sage, cedar, lavender or pinion, and other objects that have been added by the wearer because they are considered spiritually significant. Most medicine bags contain a quartz crystal. Quartz energy resonates with all the energies of the physical body and is considered a remarkable healing stone. It connects you to your spiritual self.

Other items you might like in your own medicine bag are items that may have a special attraction or resonance within your life. Some examples might be a special shell you found at the seashore, a feather you found, a piece of a pine tree or a juniper berry that holds meaning for you. We often meet up with items that just seem to be waiting for us to pick them up to carry them home, just to discover that we don't know what to do with them afterwards. This is one place to give them a home close to your heart. The essence of these special items creates an energy in your medicine bag; that energy is the force that represents you. So by creating a medicine bag and wearing it close to your heart you are connecting with your spiritual self who is the authentic you. And it will always remind you of who you are.

Your medicine bag is a holy item for you and should never be opened by anyone else. It contains your own sacred items, those that help you heal, those that bring you protection, and those items that connect you with your guides or angels. Something that represents the power of your totem animal, an animal that you closely identify with and feel a kinship for as I do with the elephant, can be put inside.

I carry many things in my tiny medicine bag. I recently met with a group of healers who laughed at me for having such a small medicine bag! Mine is only about 1 inch by 1½ inches! But its importance lies not in its size, but in its contents. My own medicine bag contains items that I can use for healing others on the spot. I carry Jojoba, a plant grown in the southwest for healing skin infections, bug bites and rashes, and the herb Feverfew to ease fevers. I carry a Moonstone for healing trauma and a small piece of Serpentine that heals all kinds of internal disorders. I carry a small ostrich feather to heal any kind of spiritual negativity, a seagull feather to remove any lesions or other intrusions upon the body and a hair from my totem animal, the elephant.

I also carry The Three Sisters: a kernel of corn, a dried bean and a squash seed that connect me to the abundance and healing of Mother Earth. So the medicine bag I carry is a healing bag. I might remove a single item or in an emergency situation, use the whole bag. When visiting someone who is sick, I may lay my bag upon the illness or broken leg, for example. It works!

Medicine bags can be as small as 1 inch by 1 inch or as large as 30 inches in length. They are typically made of leather. A pouch for this purpose can be purchased at most metaphysical stores. You can also make your own from a piece of hide or natural colored canvas. The outside of your bag should be a natural color or earth tone such as tan. You can decorate the outside of your bag with symbols or drawings of animals or leaves; whatever feels right in your heart. Before placing your items in your bag, take a moment to bless them and realize their meaning in your life and why you wish to carry them with you in this way. Bless Mother Earth and her creatures for providing these sacred objects for you.

Consider that when you carry this medicine bag, each item included within represents your own power to heal, to guide and to protect others. This is your connection to your spiritual nature. Carrying this medicine bag will increase your awareness of your own sacredness as the bag also becomes sacred.

As you go through life, you may find other things you will want to add to this medicine bag. If you wear it and add to it throughout the years, it will become a spiritual scrapbook of your life, your travels, your achievements, and who you really are. It is a wonderful thing to hand down to your grandchildren when they are able to truly understand its meaning and respect its value.

17. "What is a Prayer Tree?"

There are many ways to solidify our intentions of healing for others and ourselves. The Hopi Indians have Bahos, the Tibetans have Prayer Flags, and other Shamanic cultures have various types of physical representations of the prayers and intentions of their people, such as prayer sticks and prayer trees. A prayer tree is a Shamanic way of physically sending prayers and intentions into the spiritual.

A prayer tree can be created by just one person or by a group of people to represent a common prayer. To create a prayer tree one must find a large branch or heavy stick with several branches. This branch will represent all trees as the Tree Of Life. Plant the prayer tree upright by digging a hole or propping up the branch with rocks and stones.

Consider carefully where you will plant this tree and thank the ground for providing the perfect location.

Representations of the prayers are then tied to the prayer tree. The prayers can be pieces of ribbon, cloth, feathers, twine or any object that represents the meaning of the prayer. If the prayer tree is done in community, each person should have the opportunity to tie their prayer to the prayer tree. Always thank the prayer object for allowing itself to be used in this sacred manner. These objects are the way we ask the Universe manifested to assist us in bringing our prayers to the One Spirit.

Often verbal prayers are recited, and poetry, songs, and even drumming and rattling may accompany the ceremony of attaching the prayer objects to the tree. It is important to be specific in your intentions and deliberate in choosing the prayer objects to use. It is with intent that effects take place.

A simple prayer at the conclusion of the constructing of a prayer tree might be:

"We (I) ask this Prayer Tree to take these prayers offered here today to Creator and bring Creator's peace, healing, joy and successful completion to our requests as is best for the most perfect outcome for our higher selves. We (I) thank you for your help and Beauty today. Aho"

18. "Why are there so many different kinds of medicine wheels?"

"Different books vary on medicine wheels. Is the compilation of the information different for each culture, country, tribe and clan, etc.? If so, where do we truly begin?"

There are many different ways to do medicine wheels. Also, opinions on the medicine wheel are just as varied. Different cultures do medicine wheels differently, based on each culture's traditions. What I have found is that it is best to decide for yourself the placement of the items on the medicine wheel according to your own rationale or reasons. I don't think Spirit cares. I think the medicine wheel is a prayer. You create a medicine wheel to represent yourself and the intentions you wish to bring to Spirit. We know the power of a circle. We know the power of the four directions: North, South, East and West. We symbolize our prayer intentions by using totems in the four directions; if we are building the medicine wheel as a prayer for ourselves, we can put our own totems in the four directions.

Medicine wheels can be made out of anything. The simplest medicine wheel is four pinecones to represent the four directions and a stone in the center to represent our intention, our prayer. A little more elaborate is 12 pinecones around the circle with 3 stones in the middle. More elaborate yet is a talisman for the four totems that represent you in the four directions and a quartz stone in the center for your intentions. Even more elaborate is a talisman of 12 totems with the four directions represented by the four totems traditionally used in these places, your own totem talismans as the other nine points and a talisman that represents your intention in the center. It can be as simple or elaborate as you wish. For a personal medicine wheel I would use talismans that represented the qualities I wanted to achieve or that I was praying for per the information given here. But again a simple pinecone representing these things is fine. It is in the understanding of what you are doing that the medicine wheel is created.

As an example, for the east I might have a token of the animal totem that represents the strength I need to overcome a spiritual challenge. Remember that the old ones knew the spiritual qualities of our animal brothers by heart. We might have to look them up. There are many good places to look them up given in the 101 Course's lesson on totems.

North
This direction gives you wise counsel and reminds you when to speak and when to listen. It also reminds you to be grateful for every blessing every day.

West
This direction leads to your personal truth and inner answers. It also shows you the path to your goals.

East
This is the direction of spiritual challenges, inspirations and visions. It is a path to illumination.

South
This direction protects the child within and reminds us when to be humble and when to trust, so that innocence will be balanced in our personalities.

Some medicine wheels are built permanently. Some people build a medicine wheel in their house or in their yard and keep them forever. I would put more elaboration into this kind of wheel. I would take my time and use those talismans I had been given by my power animals, put them in the most appropriate place on the medicine wheel, and use the talismans I have been give that most represent my life and life goals in the center. This would be a personal medicine wheel.

Some medicine wheels are built temporarily such as on a beach at low tide or in a forest. They are usually built with natural materials that speak to you from that place such as shells, pinecones, and things from nature. Again, be sure to have the four directions represented and your intention in the center.

Always open a wheel by welcoming the four directions, praying your intentions and then giving thanks for the prayer's manifestation or success. I like to sing my power song or drum, rattle or dance. Close the medicine wheel as you opened it and leave it there. The old ones say you should build an outdoor medicine wheel in the morning and when the sun passes over it, the spirit of the eagle carries your intention to Spirit on the sun. Beautiful!

Here are some ways of welcoming the four directions:
Facing east:
"Spirit of the east where light comes from and the element of air, enlighten me."

Facing south;
"Spirit of the south where the sun is the strongest, and element of fire, let me seek."

Facing west;
"Spirit of the west where the sun sets and element of water, give me strength."

Facing north;
"Spirit of the north where the sun rests and element of earth, give me knowledge."

So there are many ways to build a medicine wheel. Most ancient cultures had or have some sort of medicine wheel ceremony. But you must show respect for these ancient ceremonies and understand please that in some Native American traditions the Medicine Wheel is so sacred that only certain people are allowed to do their ceremony. The power of the medicine wheel lies not so much in the physical symbols used as in the spiritual purpose and intent.

19. "What do animals tell us?"

In Shamanism there is much importance given to animals as guides, totems and helpers. This is more than just having a favorite animal or being attracted to butterflies, for example. Shamans have used animals as a source of diagnosis in healing and counseling all around the world throughout recorded history.

Each animal has its own nature and its own traits. Each is a representation of a specific power, such as strength for the lion or speed for the jaguar. By learning about animal strengths or powers, a Shaman comes to an understanding of why people are attracted to certain "favorite" animals and repulsed by others. These attractions and repulsions actually become tools that tell the Shaman what is needed or missing in a person's life.

There was a woman who, no matter how she tried, kept missing the boat, missing out on opportunities that would have brought her the abundance and connections she needed to succeed. In hindsight, she could see every instance in which she had failed to recognize the chance to get ahead. It was very frustrating for her but she could not find a way to break out of this rut.

When asked what animal she most feared, she related an experience she had as a child with a horse. She was introduced to a friend's horse that was very high-spirited. When she reached out her little hand, the horse bit it, causing much trauma for the child and a lot of consternation for her mother. And since that time, the horse had represented fear for this woman.

As we look at the power of the horse, we see that it is a prey animal. That means it is usually a source of food for some other animal. So it is keenly aware of what is going on around it at all times. One quick move, one strange sound and the horse will perk up its ears and be on the alert for what is happening, ready to run if it feels any danger. Horses also watch out for one another; if one horse senses danger, the whole herd is willing to move as one, away from the apparent threat.

So, examining this woman from a Shamanic perspective, we see that she is not aware of what is around her and she is afraid of the power represented by the horse, the power to be keenly aware of her own situation at all times. By dealing with her fear of horses, we can allow her once again to become aware of her surroundings, to prick her ears up and take full advantage of the opportunities around her.

Similarly, we can use the characteristics of those animals we are most attracted to as clues about powers we have or would like to have. Recently a student became interested in developing her spiritual gifts and stated that she was attracted to the snake. Certainly, it is an unusual animal to attract the favor of a woman! She just seemed to think about the snake more often than any other animal and it had only been this way for the past year or so.

When we look at the snake we see that it represents the power of transformation. The snake can shed its skin and create a new one within a short time. It has always been a symbol of power and has even been regarded as the mother of all life. The life energy called Kundalini is often described as a snake rising up the spinal column to bring enlightenment.

So for this woman, the snake was showing her that, yes, it is time to begin developing her healing abilities and to take charge of her own power to help others. As she progresses, other animals will become her favorites, and those animals will have significance in her life, too.

It is said that we carry 12 totem animals in our lives. Usually there are four animals that stay with us constantly and which represent the powers that are inherent in our spirit- in the past, presently, and eternally. The other eight totems represent life-changing events or growth cycles as we move along this path of life, learning and practicing what we have learned. If you pay attention to the animals you favor most and those you dislike, you can learn many things about your true desires and how to attain them.

20. "When you refer to the talismans (i.e. stones, feathers, etc.) being presented to us, do you mean on our inner journeys or in the physical world?"

Talismans come from many places. Sometimes we find something significant as we are out for a walk in nature or while shopping. We are drawn to an object and feel a connection to it. Then it is our responsibility to find out about that connection through prayer, meditation and insights. Just leave the question open in your heart, "What is the meaning of this gift to me?" Usually your guides will answer the question for you when you are ready for the answer.

The other way a talisman is presented to us is through an insight or in meditation or prayer, during which we see something given to us in a visualization. Perhaps an elder gives you a feather in your dream. Later you are walking in the woods and you see a feather in physical form and realize that it is the same feather you were given by that elder. Or maybe you see a stone and recognize it as the feather from your elder. It does not have to have the same face in the outer worlds as it does in the inner worlds but it will have the same energy signature, the same feeling.

Sometimes we are attracted to a talisman that is meant for others. I may be walking in the woods, praying for someone who is sick and I come across a stone that just attracts me. I pick up the stone and feel if it is for the person I am praying for, and I know if it is or is not, in my heart. I would give the stone to that person as an aid for answering the prayer I was intending.

Sometimes Shaman Elder Maggie leaves a gift in your path for you! It might be a stick or feather or a rock or even a small memento you found in a store that speaks of Shaman Elder's love and healing for you! And you can leave gifts for others as well. It is the intention and the emotion behind that intention that manifests the talisman.

21. "What is a talking stick?"

A talking stick is a very beautifully decorated stick used by tribal members in Native American cultures to honor the speaker holding it with undivided attention and respect. When an opinion or decision is to be made by a group, it is passed to each member in turn. The person holding the stick "has the floor" and the freedom to speak their truth without being interrupted. When that person is finished talking, it is then handed to the next person, who will also have the opportunity to speak his or her truth. Most decisions are made after all the elders have a chance to say what they believe to be true. In short, the talking stick allows each person the honor to say what he or she wants to say, with respect. It is a great instrument to use in your home with your family. Try it with your kids!

22. "Do most people require physical symbols to accept that someone is able to perform a healing and to display that the healing act has been accomplished?"

Oh my goodness, YES! And Shamans know this very well. For me to do a soul extraction from here and tell you in an email that it has been done, does not compare to me coming to your house, having you lie down on a table and pulling hidden chicken guts out of my sleeve while telling you that I removed this sickness from your body.

Shamans count on symbolism to send home the healing! In third world countries where some people cannot read and write, they need something to hold onto in order to believe. They need to drink the blood of a chicken, be washed in the sacred river or be given an amulet or voodoo doll. Why, right in our grocery stores you can buy a candle to burn to the saint of your choice for a favor.

It is human nature to want a symbol that can be held and seen, especially to show that something tangible has certainly occurred. We tend to believe with our eyes and not with our hearts and souls. We can be healed through prayer but not be able to accept that healing until the priest comes to our hospital bed and puts oil on our foreheads.

How I wish that people would not have this kind of "seeing is believing" attitude! But I don't think we will ever reach that place. So the Shaman understands this and is willing to give symbols if they are necessary to effect a healing. What kind of symbols? Perhaps the Shaman would give you a leaf of a healing plant, or a stone, amulet, or a feather; perhaps a picture of a Saint or Ascended Master is chosen. Maybe something more profound needs to be done, such as painting the patient's body, washing his face or tying a bandage around his leg. The symbol can be anything that reaffirms the healing for the patient. If you know your patient, you know what symbol to give. I think that Reiki healing would be more widespread and spoken of in a higher manner if we gave people some symbol of Reiki when offering a healing.

But as long as people only believe what they see, the Shaman will use symbols to allow the person to see their healing and have something to show that it has occurred. And the Shaman will charge money for that healing because money is another symbol of validation for most people. The client may only feel the healing has value if he has traded something of value for it. Healings given for free are often worthless to the receiver. Again, this is just human nature and I wish that this were not true. But in general, one way to get the client to believe in the healing is to give it value by charging for it in money or barter. All Shamans know this and do this. And doctors, lawyers and grocers do this, too!

We have to work within the common reality in which we live. And in the common reality is the belief in symbols as powerful tokens of healing, understanding and growth. Symbols are also used as badges of accomplishment and authority, among other things. So we use the tools at hand to do the work we need to do. Don't be obsessed with it but count it as a tool in your practice.

4   Safety and Protection

23. "How do I stay safe in this reality and in others?"

Let's talk about the importance of centering and grounding. Never, ever journey without your spirit animals, your allies. If your allies don't journey with you then you are not meant to go. Remember – these spirit animals represent a higher force that is looking out for you.

Also, as we begin to journey we are shining an incredible bright light for anyone to see. Certain entities see that light and see that you are a novice and try to get you to do their bidding mostly by pretending to be someone they are not. You can recognize that they are not who they say they are by their energy signatures. You can feel that there is something wrong; that this energetic being or entity is not who he says he is. Pay attention to your gut feelings.

The entities know where power is in these Inner Planes. And sometimes they need your power to get what they want. And again it comes down to- what is your intention for going on this journey? You must have an intention set firmly in your mind and you must not let anything take you off track from that intention.

24. "Can you give me a surefire way to be grounded and protected?"

When you take a breath in, breathe in from the ground, from Mother Earth, from the roots of yourself and the trees, the grass, the rivers, and the seas. Breathe in grounding and balance that Mother Earth gives us gladly. Breathe in from your feet all the way to above your head.

When you breathe out, breathe down from the top of your head. Breathe down the love of Creator from above. Breathe down to your feet all the love, protection, and guidance freely given to you from Spirit. Feel it coming down through your head all the way to your toes as you exhale. Let it fill you up. Then inhale again and let the grounding of Mother Earth fill you up from your feet to above your head. Just do this constantly. Be aware of it. It is like two spirals of energy. And they meet in your solar plexus, your third chakra, forming a figure 8. Feel the energies going up and coming down like two vortices. I picture the one from Mother Earth as spinning counterclockwise and the one from Spirit spinning clockwise. You can let me know what direction they spin in for you.

This exercise gathers etheric energy or chi into your energetic self. This chi or etheric energy promotes healing, balance and peace. That is how valuable this exercise is. How easy is it to bring power into your life? This easy!

Just do this constantly. You will really feel filled with power, protection, grounding and a strong connection to guidance. Sure you will forget as you busy yourself with other things, but when you remember just keep doing it.

Then imagine yourself surrounded by a bubble of protection as though you are standing inside an eggshell. The outside of the eggshell can be white, a mirror or Teflon depending on what you prefer. Mine is made of a Teflon-type material that lets in good energy but filters out any negative energy. It will not allow negative energetic cords to connect to it. Now fill the inside of the eggshell where you are standing with pure violet light energy that comes down from Creator from above. Let this beautiful violet light fill the bubble and bathe you in peace and love from Creator. Just feel this for a few moments and enjoy it.

"I thank Creator, my guides and helpers, the angels and all loving beings for your protection. I go in peace and love."

25. "Should I fear studying Shamanism?"

We are taught fear from birth. Our parents used fear to control us. If you have raised children yourself, you know that you may have used fear to scare the kids into doing what you wanted them to do. Likewise, fear is frequently the controller in school; you may have been told that you were going to be punished if you didn't do things the way your teachers and the ones in charge wanted you to. Staying after school, detention, the principal's office, failing grades...all these were about fear.

So by the time we finish school, many of us are totally controlled by fear, as it has become the biggest part of our lives. Then we go to work. We learn to fear coming in late, displeasing the boss, not doing a super job every day, taking too long a lunch break and all kinds of other work-related fears are set into motion. So fear then can dominate our work life. Then we get married. And we can use fear to control each other. I won't love you if you.... displease me in any way. Get that supper on the table in time or I will be angry. Mow that lawn or I will shame you to the neighbors. And the fear mounts. Fear of anger many times can become the control in a relationship as well.

Wow! We are fear-based people, aren't we! How sad! At what point do we get to breathe??? No wonder we are unhappy. What a rotten way to live!

And who has time nowadays to unravel 30 or 40 years of fear-based thinking? It is easier to take Prozac than to go to a psychological therapist. It is easier to medicate than to break the chain. And it takes breaking the chain to find freedom, happiness and power.

What would you like to do? How precious is your freedom to you? How badly do you want to be happy? How much is your personal power worth to you?

Taking my course in Shamanism requires one to accept his or her own power. It teaches you where it is and shows the way. The course teaches you how to be a hunter and a warrior, and to work with the tools that have been given to you already but that you may be afraid to use (because many have discouraged you from doing so). Why did they discourage you? Because if you learn to use your Creator-given tools, no one will any longer be able to control you with fear.

When we truly take back our power, no person can have power over us again.

When we truly take back our power, we become responsible for everything that happens to us. We can make wonderful things happen in our lives. We are no longer under the influence of anyone else's poor plans for our lives.

Who knows you better than you do? Why do you let others decide what is best for you? Only you know what is best for you. Step up and make your choices; take responsibility for your choices and watch those fear-based controllers run for the hills. Those who were controlling you will leave. Why should they stay if they can't touch you anymore!?

Believe me, it's a very freeing feeling and all it takes is a choice, a different way of living.

Shamanism teaches you to reclaim your power; that you are strong and that yes, you do create your own reality. Shamanism also expects you to accept responsibility for yourself and for your actions and consequences. It is wonderful to be in charge of your own life! It is great to know that whatever you want in life is yours with the proper knowledge, the sincere intent and the correct emotional control. Shamanism gives you these skills. It is a great thing!

What if I am afraid of studying Shamanism?

Fear is a choice you can make. The other choice is freedom. Letting someone control you leads to fear, whereas taking control of yourself leads to freedom.

Come walk with a Shaman and learn how to take control of yourself and experience the freedom to have anything you really want out of life.

26. "I have visions. Is that good?"

Sometimes what we see can be happening or about to happen in other realities besides this one. There are other realities that look very much like this one does, physically. They are called alternate realities. Jim Carrey made a movie called *The Truman Show* in which everything about his life was staged inside a bubble. Remember that movie? And he tried to sail away in a boat, but the boat stopped at the edge of the bubble. He then realized that his world was not real. Some realities are *that close* to our own.

It was a pleasant day outside and I had left the door open to allow some fresh air into the house. As I was standing in my living room cleaning the rugs, I looked up and there, outside my front door and down the front walk, were horses and buggies going by in the road outside. There were houses across the street that weren't there before, tall brownstones, and as I looked, a man walked by in a top hat. There was a picket fence in front of my house that was not there before. I looked back into my living room and then back out the door, and this scene continued playing. I just stood there mesmerized, watching for a long time, maybe 15 minutes, while carriages and people walked by my house. I saw a milk truck drive by as some kids in knickers ran by playing with a hoop. I looked at myself dressed in my jeans and saw my living room just as it has always been, and then look out the door again to observe this other reality lingering there. It persisted until I left the living room and then returned again, at which point it was gone.

We are just a sheet of paper away from other realities. Sometimes we are more connected to other realities than to this one. Some people prefer to live in other realities; they are kept in insane asylums. It is not that they are insane; it is that they are more connected to other places and other times. If someone would study this phenomenon and do the research, we might be able to help these "insane" people. I have come very close to choosing another reality myself. I was really tempted to stay in another alternate reality, which was so much more loving than this one. I had to struggle with myself, to tell myself that I am here for a purpose, so that I could even consider being and staying here.

Even now I get sad thinking about it. Perhaps this is one place depression comes from.

I hear from people every day that are slipping into and out of this reality. They don't completely slip out but they feel disconnected to this reality and cannot control when this shift occurs. It is hard to tell people that they should remain grounded here when some part of them knows that it is better "over there".

But it's not favorable or advantageous for people to be slipping back and forth without control, either. One guy was losing his job over it. A lady was losing her kids over it. We all want the better world. Somewhere inside we have seen it or felt it and we all know about it. Although it might not be on a conscious level, most of us are having a hard time finding a real reason to stay here. The ones who can stay here the best are the warriors, the healers, and the ones who like to fight and make a difference, the champions for a cause.

I found that for me, either I choose to become a healer or wind up in an asylum. Do you remember the sainted nuns who would cloister themselves in abbeys for their whole lives? They would never see anyone but the priest, who would bring them one meal a day. Their lives were spent in prayer for the church, the town, and the country. Believe me, that is one way to live in a better world. They were seldom in this reality.

I see that this world is being populated more and more by people who have chosen to be healers, warriors, hunters and Shamans, who do battle to save this world, this reality. We were definitely put here for a purpose, no matter how odious this reality might be. We chose to be here and to make a difference. I continue telling myself this to ground myself here, in this reality.

My point to you is that there are many realities and you may be picking up on any one of them at any time. How can you know if what you're experiencing is from this place or another? Only through experience, practice, keeping a log and recording the results.

Learn about other realities as well, so that you can recognize them better in your visions. I saw a whole star system collapse when I was 24. I had a series of visions of this incredible implosion of the cosmos. It was very scary for me to see, as I thought it was this universe. It did happen but it happened a million, billion miles away in another time.

I am not saying that what you are seeing is not for here and now. I have no way to say that. I am not here to judge what you see. You are the best judge of what you see. You have to learn to interpret as well as see. Remember that Edgar Cayce could only "see" when he was in a light self-trance, lying on his couch. Someone else had to write down everything he said. The same is true about Seth. But you and I don't have that luxury. We have to do both.

You know what might be terrific? If you could find someone willing to write down the verbal dictation of your visions, or maybe you yourself could verbally record them. You would have to learn to say what you see out loud, which might take some practice to become comfortable doing. Regardless of the method you choose to record your visions, I want to encourage you to pursue this gift. We need visionaries.

27. "How do you communicate with your guides and teachers?"

For me, in my daily sessions, I approach a council fire in a place where it is always night. There are starry skies and a blazing inviting fire because I love those things. If you love a fountain and noon time, that could be your council setting. My guides are sitting around the fire in the dim light. I often see them chatting with each other when I arrive. Each of my guides is not present for every council fire. Sometimes there are only one or two teachers or guides there. Sometimes, though, all 12 of my teachers and guides are there. I sit on the ground on the south side of the fire circle. They sit up on logs lain on their sides, like seats. I approach the circle with reverence, respect and humility because these are ancient spirits, ancient souls who know so very much that I am like a little child in their presence. I greet them and they nod or speak to me. I feel great love for me in this circle!

Sometimes I just sit and listen to what they are talking about. I feel honored that they let me listen. I listen hard and try to understand and remember all that I hear. Sometimes I don't understand anything. Sometimes I understand but forget it all too quickly.

Sometimes I have a question for them about me or about a client or a student. When I feel that it is okay to interrupt their dialogue, usually they pause and look at me as if to say, "Okay, go ahead now", and I ask that question.

Sometimes they think about it and give me several suggestions as to what I might do or consider doing about the issue. Sometimes they say in unison what to do. Sometimes they ask me what I think I should do or say, or what I believe. Sometimes they tell me to come back later. In the latter case, I figure that the answer was not mine to have at that time; either I was not ready to hear it, or it was not ready to be done.

I don't ask many questions. My job is to listen and learn at the council fire.

Sometimes as I am sitting and listening, one of my teachers will begin to talk to me. I may be asked some questions or asked to speak my truth about a certain subject or method of healing or even about a client or student, as they know who I am working with. Sometimes I am given an assignment. It can be anything from finding a feather to going to the park to doing one of the exercises in the course. It can be to say something to someone, to solve a riddle, to find a stone or to work with a color or symbol. It can be anything. I have been given so many assignments over the years.

On a recent assignment, just as an example for you, I had to fly to New York to speak at a gathering and was told by my council that this would be a learning experience for me. Even the airport would be a learning experience. Well that made me a little nervous to say the least as I am imagining everything under the sun. But I was being very aware. My planes were all delayed and the trip took 13 hours instead of 6. But what I noticed, what I was thankfully aware enough to see, was that in every airport and every plane, all the people I saw were people I had seen before! It was as if there were 144,000 people in the world and I kept seeing them over and over. Or there were 144,000 people in my reality and no more! Isn't that neat! It is really odd to sit in an airport, look around and recognize everyone there!

Now, I kept watching for this phenomenon. And at one point I was going on a side trip with some friends to where they wanted to go. So I was just along for the ride. And we went to a beautiful canyon where people were swimming in the river and sliding on the beautiful, slippery rocks. Being acutely aware of everything around me, I looked at the people here and realized that I had never seen any of them before! They were not part of my 144,000! They were my friend's 144,000. I was in her reality now. How wonderful!

Now, that experience came directly from my guides and teachers. My point in sharing it is that your guides and teachers use many ways to teach you. Sometimes they speak to you. Sometimes they show you things. Sometimes they set up experiences in your life that, if you can be aware enough, you can learn from. Even after 50 years, my guides and teachers are still teaching me. This is the place of real teaching, not in a book, not in a manuscript, this is the real teaching for you! Everything you need to learn and more can be received from this council you now have. So appreciate what you have here.

Respect these guides and teachers, and learn to work with them. They can teach you things you cannot even imagine about energy, science, human beings, healing, everything! And far better than you can read in a book. They will teach you soul retrieval when you are ready to learn it. Yes, I will teach you too. They will teach you all the skills you need to be a healer in this world. That is why they are here for you. That is why. Do not waste them. Do not tie them and gag them and put them in a corner only to be brought out when you feel like it. Do not hide from them. And do not abuse them.

They will not stay where they are not wanted. Remember that they will never go against your free-will choice. If you do not want them to teach you, then they surely won't. But they won't stick around either. The worst that can happen is that you force your council to go away because you do not want them, because you do not want to have the determination and commitment to learn, grow and walk your path. Yes, they do require some effort on your part; a willingness on your part to learn and respect what they are giving you. And you can force them to go away.

You can even allow in a fake panel of inner world beings who look like guides but who don't teach you anything. They are like puppets you create, you manipulate, and you control, who only say what you already know and what you want to hear. It is a puppet theatre, not a council. And you can set up this illusion for yourself and live in it for as long as you like. It won't make you happy and it won't do you any good. It will constantly frustrate you. This is the worst that can happen and I know you will not do this to yourself.

Now, you probably want to know how to tell if your council is real or just some puppet panel you made up. First of all, you probably have a puppet panel if you are kidding yourself and you are not facing this work seriously. Second, if you are not facing yourself honestly. Third, if you are only reading the material and not doing the work. As I said, your council is not here if you don't want to work with them.

Your council feels like your place; you are loved by these guides. They have come of their own free will to help you walk your path. They never force you to do things. They never demand that you do something. Everything they offer you is uplifting, insightful, and usually things you would never think of yourself. All they tell you is always good, from Source. They don't pander to your emotions. They don't upset you, excite you or get you riled up in any emotional way. A puppet council does that all the time. You can always test the spirits (www.shamanelder.com/testingthespirits.html) but you already know within your heart if you are honestly willing to work with this wonderful guidance from Creator, or not.

5 Traditional Shamanic Wisdom

28. "Can you explain what 'grace' is?"

Grace is a Christian word that, as you said in your letter, describes something that is bestowed upon us by God for doing good works and being a good person. The prayer "Hail Mary, full of grace..." mentions this quality. It seems to be a distant and unattainable quality or endowment that we earn, according to the church, by virtue.

Various interpretations of 'virtue' have been proposed over the ages. Classical Greek philosophers considered the foremost virtues to be prudence, temperance, courage, and justice. Early Christian Church theologians adopted these virtues and considered them to be equally important to all people, whether they were Christian or not.

St. Paul gave us the three chief virtues as love, hope, and faith. Christian Church authorities called them 'The Three Theological Virtues' because they believed the virtues were not natural to man in his fallen state, but were conferred upon him at Baptism.

I found this shocking explanation of 'the virtues' in the writings of St. Augustine:

"In this world of iniquity, they are a few gleams of hope in the mire of our shameful indulgences."

The Contrary Virtues came from the Psychomachia "Battle for the Soul", an epic poem written by Prudentius. Practicing these virtues: humility, kindness, abstinence, chastity, patience, liberality and diligence is intended to protect one against the Seven Deadly Sins: humility against pride, kindness against envy, abstinence against gluttony, chastity against lust, patience against anger, liberality against greed, and diligence against sloth.

The Seven Heavenly Virtues combine the Four Cardinal Virtues: prudence, temperance, fortitude (or courage) and justice, with the Theological Virtues: faith, hope, and charity.

The Christian Church assembled a list of seven good works. They are: feed the hungry, give drink to the thirsty, give shelter to strangers, clothe the naked, visit the sick, minister to prisoners, and bury the dead. But now, let's look at grace or goodness from another perspective.

The Seven Virtues of the Bushido Warrior were created for the Traditional Samurai Warrior. All Samurai lived by these 7 virtues. These virtues were required in their physical training and were considered their code of conduct for everyday living, making them soldiers. They were the reason the Samurai were so highly respected in their society.

I list them here for you with their interpretation according to the Makoto Ryu Karate-Do Association's 'Seven Virtue System'.

Virtue No. 1 "Gi": Right decision, fair and equal. Gi is the ability to make the correct decisions with confidence, to be fair and equal towards all people no matter what color, race, gender or age. This virtue is the ability to make a decision, respecting all equally.

Virtue No. 2 "Yu": Valor & Courage. Yu is created as the student progresses in rank and as his skills become more fluent and based on reflex. The student gains confidence in himself, knowing he can handle any situation that presents itself. This virtue is the ability to handle any situation.

Virtue No. 3 "Jin": Benevolence, Compassion & Generosity. Jin is the humble virtue in which the student is discouraged from using his/her new-founded skills for bigotry and domination.

This virtue works together with "Gi". This virtue is important in preventing arrogance within oneself.

Virtue No. 4 "Rei": The Proper Behavior, Courtesy & Respect. This virtue makes the student aware of the principle of the Yin and the Yang, that one cannot exist without the other. The teacher cannot be a teacher without a student; therefore, both are equal in their own right. This virtue is integral in the ability to have respect for all.

Virtue No. 5 "Makoto": Honesty, Honor & Morality. This virtue is best described as "one must be honest to one's self before he can be honest with anyone else". Cheating and lying is an acceptance of failure and creates a false environment for the student. This virtue is the ability to do things the best we can.

Virtue No. 6 "Meiyo": Success, Honor and Glory. This virtue follows the student as he/she becomes a better warrior within himself or herself. Honor, success and glory follow a positive attitude. This virtue is frequently sought after, but can only come as the result of correct behavior.

Virtue No. 7 "Chungi": Devotion and Loyalty, Dedication. This virtue is the foundation of all the virtues. Without dedication and loyalty to the task at hand, the desired outcome cannot be achieved. This virtue supports all success.

In Shamanic cultures, living your life and strengthening your character according to these virtues are what make you impeccable, a good warrior, a good hunter, a person who lives in his/her own power. And by living your life within these precepts you gain "grace" or "gong", which is the result of the effort to develop chi.

The Shaman is one who has the ability to make a decision, respecting all equally. The true Shaman has the ability to handle any situation. The true Shaman uses benevolence, compassion and mercy to remove any traces of arrogance from him or herself. The true Shaman lives with proper behavior, courtesy and respect for all created things. The true Shaman does everything to the best of his or her ability. The true Shaman knows that correct behavior and positive attitude lead to success in all things. The true Shaman is completely dedicated and devoted to the spirit imbued in all things created.

As I have often said, there is one thing that humans can gain in this life experience and take with them from lifetime to lifetime, and this attribute is grace or gong. It is this grace that brings us ever closer to At-One-Ment with the Source. The Buddha had achieved this union in his lifetime and Buddhists recognize that once it is attained it is never taken away. They look for the Buddha's reincarnation, having an elaborate system to find the Buddha in each lifetime. You may have seen one of many movies showing us how they gather young boys together that have the characteristics they require. They present the little boys with certain possessions of the previous incarnation to see if he recognizes his belongings. The point is that once these qualities of a Buddha are attained in a lifetime, they are never lost.

So grace is a drink of water and we are the cup. We start out with only the grace we obtained in other lives. We practice virtue, Christian or Bushido, to gather grace and to try to fill our cups more while we are here. A person who can completely fill their cup in his or her lifetime reaches enlightenment or At-One-Ment, which is complete union with Source.

In my opinion, Jesus too had attained this At-One-Ment before he ever came to this planet. He showed us how to walk this earth with a complete union with Father. If He can do it, so can we. He was not about guilt or sin. He showed us the way to walk in virtue 24/7. He showed us the way to attain grace so we could be in complete At-One-Ment with God. He taught us love. He also said that we could, with love, in his Father's Name, do what He had done here and more. And that includes healing the sick and raising the dead.

For the Shaman, all the virtues are the path to grace. It is grace, chi, or gong, that we are here to obtain. Practicing 'The

Virtues' increases grace. It is a way of living, more than a condition of life.

I believe that we are a part of Source. And Source is a part of us. Source is completely in us, in every molecule and atom. We are completely Source. But we are like an atom on the nail of a finger. Source is so much more than just us. All of us together that have ever been or will be might fill one fingernail on the hand of Source. To find complete Unity in consciousness, to fill consciously with Source and be in Source and to realize it would be the definition of the Buddhist term Samadhi. This is what we are here to do. This is what grace gives us, looking at it from a Christian perspective.

So the Shaman needs to be impeccable, as flawless as he/she can be. Notice I didn't say perfect. He practices 'The Virtues' in his life to reach a state of receiving grace or chi. When he goes to the Inner Worlds, this impeccability is his power and his grace, and he shines like a searchlight there. Everyone, all the beings physically manifested or unmanifested, see him coming as he shines so brightly, and they all want that light for themselves. But he is also shining so brightly that they recognize his grace and his power, and they are frightened of him. When the Shaman does a soul retrieval from this state, he doesn't get much argument from the Inner World beings. He doesn't have to wage war or fight dragons. He uses his power, to be a benevolent and powerful practitioner with mastery of the Inner Worlds and love in his heart. Love is stronger than anything in the Inner Worlds. Virtue is made of love. Read 'The Virtues' again and see the connection between each of them and love.

Power.

So we came into this life carrying the grace we have gained in other places and other lifetimes. This is our power. We come here already having this power. We are here to gain more grace and more power. You have power; a lot of power. In some churches, we are taught to think we have no power, no grace. But we are taught to practice 'The Virtues' and that, at the least, is a good teaching. The church may have taken away our power but still let us have the key to gaining grace. Of course they told us we could never be virtuous enough to gain grace, but that is the rhetoric of the church hierarchy trying to keep people under their control. The answer is yes, we can gain grace.

So grace is power? Absolutely. And what is grace? Love. So love is power? Absolutely! What is love? Source. So Source is power? Yes. The Source that is in each one of us is our power. The love that is in each one of us is our power. The grace that is in each one of us according to our virtue, is our power. "Oh, is power variable?" you may ask. Does the amount of our power vary depending on our grace or virtue? Yes.

OK, so what about "bad" people who seem to have lots of power? I've said that everyone comes here with the grace they have already accumulated. So everybody comes here with a certain amount of power. That power can be used for good or bad. "Bad" people are using their accumulated grace from previous lifetimes but in a self-centered way this time. It will not be taken away from them, but they are not increasing their grace here as they are not being virtuous. So yes, they have power and they choose to use it badly. This free-will choice is always yours to use in whichever way you choose.

I hope I have explained what grace is, what virtue is, what power is, where it comes from, and how the Shaman uses his grace and increases his grace. It is kind of a new teaching, maybe different than you have heard before. It is my condensation of views from the Christian and Buddhist faiths. I wrote a paper about it many years ago. I don't have the paper anymore, but I hope this sheds some new light on the subject for you.

29. "What is the deal with 'good versus bad'?"

So I caught your attention with the most argued about and unresolved issue on the planet. Good versus bad, or 'Is there such a thing as good and bad?'. There are at least 30 camps on this issue. As a child, I used to believe in good versus bad. Modern karmic teachings show that good gets repaid as well as bad. Almost all theology pins its basis on "good versus bad".

But energy is energy; it is not good energy or bad energy. We are energy. I became even less convinced of good versus bad as I studied Hawaiian Shamanism several years ago. The respected elders in Hawaii teach that everyone you meet is just showing you a side of yourself. So to be a healer and have clients come to me for healing means I have a lot of healing to do myself! Wow! That slapped me in the face! So every time I encounter a nasty person, am I being shown that I am nasty? And every time I meet a "bad" person, am I being shown my badness? Well, the definition of good versus bad doesn't work in this context.

But what is being said is that everything we see, hear, taste, touch and feel is our own creation. We create our own reality and all that is in it. It seems kind of tough to take responsibility for all this muck. It is too hard for most people to swallow and hard to teach as well. We have to be extremely honest with ourselves to even get a grip on the concept. We all like to blame someone else for the "not so pretty" things in our lives. We all like to make a rut and stay in it, to not change, to just roll along with some degree of comfort and have the time to do the things we enjoy. This is what we want in life.

Why would anybody want to go beyond that? Why would anybody want to do the soul searching, the realizing, and the taking of responsibility for their entire lives? You see, "good versus bad" is a way to perpetuate the idea that you are not responsible.

There are a lot more folks out there who believe they are not responsible than those that can stand up and say, "Yes, I am unhappy because I made myself unhappy" or "I made myself sick". Many of us make excuses, blaming circumstances in our lives or other people for our unhappiness.

And I think it will always be that way. Is that bad? Yes and no. Is it bad to let someone else run your life? Does anyone know what is good for you more than you do? Well, you can see it gets complicated. I am merely pointing out the purpose of the argument about "good versus bad" and what it takes to get beyond that excuse. I address this subject thoroughly with all my students who wish to know more about it.

30. "I realize I am human but I have a hard time when it comes to forgiveness."

In each encounter with another person, accept whatever belief works for you and throw the rest away. Your reality is not anyone else's reality and what works for others may or may not work for you. It is important to see this and to discern what you will embrace and what you will not embrace, without criticism or judgment. Bless them for sharing and be who you need to be.

I was just remembering a situation in my life. My family constantly harps at me, saying "Why don't you give up that game of teaching and go get a real job?' Wow! How that affected my thoughts and actions! And my answer back was… (Get this!) "I would rather be poor and teach than be rich doing a "real job." Well, didn't that just guarantee my poverty!?! This whole issue is something for me to work on, but the important part was realizing what I believed!

Once you can get in touch with what you believe, then you can decide to keep that belief or believe something else. So I changed my reply to my family to, "Teaching *is* my regular job." I know this will make a difference in what I manifest. It is so simple, really, once you get the awareness of what you believe there is no need for forgiveness. But we don't like to look at our beliefs.

We were taught not to look. Your mom might have said, "Go to your room!" and you may have asked, "Why?" and she might have said something along the lines of "None of your business" or" Just do what I say!" Many of us have learned to do what others order and dictate without knowing why. And we do this with ourselves. We don't know why we do things, say things or even believe things. Have you ever looked to see why you are doing the job you are doing? Or why you are married to your wife, this one woman out of all the women in the world you could be married to? Have you ever looked at why you believe in God? These are the kinds of introspections that make us aware of our beliefs and why we believe them. And this is what causes us to judge anyone who does believe as we believe.

This is a good exercise to do and I recommend doing it in every area of your life. Some areas will not open up freely and those are the ones you can keep digging at over time. And there will always be beliefs popping up into your awareness. Suddenly you will realize something like, "Why do I always wear red ties? Because somebody told me they showed power. But I don't even like the color red!" And you can laugh at yourself! I often laugh out loud and decide, like this person after his realization, that yes, I can wear any color tie I want to. I'm talking about changing your beliefs by being aware of exactly what you believe. This is a lifetime job but the rewards are freedom, power, and balance.

The true Shaman is constantly doing this work. The Shaman has no time to judge you!

In the end, and I know this from experience, you will judge yourself. You will judge whether your belief system was right or wrong. Spirit does not judge. And in some ways that is even scarier than thinking God will judge you. You will judge yourself! We learn from others who have experienced death or near-death experiences that your life will flash before you at the moment of death. I know that it is slightly more than this. I died and left my body, and went into the light. I saw my life from another state, from my Buddhic body, and I saw everything I had done, everyone whom I had influenced and all the conversations I'd had, both good and bad. I saw all the experiences of my life - how they influenced me and how I influenced others. I saw what my beliefs did to me, myself, as well as to others. I instantly knew what beliefs were right and which were wrong. I saw where I got them from and who I affected with them. I saw the reasons why things happened as they did, but from a different perspective. I could see how my words affected each person I spoke to and what actions these people took as a result of my words. And all I wanted to do immediately was to ask forgiveness from everyone I had affected negatively.

We do not see what we are doing here with our judgments. But when you do see the affects of your words and thoughts and actions you too will be asking for forgiveness. I think it is better not to judge in the first place. Just know that you don't know the best thing for everyone else. You only can know what is best for you.

Another example of self-judgment after death is the case of my mother's death. At one point while she was alive, she felt she needed to take my child away from me because I was going to Colorado with my baby for a three-week vacation, which my mother believed was a very irresponsible decision on my part. When she died, she saw that I truly was going on vacation and that it was good for us to take that vacation. She realized that a lot of great bonding happened during that time. So she saw, at the moment of her death, that she had made a mistake in her actions in that situation because of her belief system. Luckily, it had no deleterious effect on anyone, except for hurt feelings all around. And I had already forgiven her for that, anyway.

(It is vitally important for us, before we leave this planet, to forgive everyone who may have harmed us in any manner. We do this for their sakes, not ours. We may leave at any moment, so it is crucial to do our forgiving now.)

I was fortunate, in that all those I had harmed had already forgiven me and I was free to go on into the Unity with Oneness. We cannot unite with Creator unless we have this forgiveness. It is the thing that separates us from Creator. Creator does not hold us separate. Creator does not judge us or cause any separation. We do. We judge ourselves and we cause our own separation from full unity in At-One-Ment.

I also should tell you the other side of the coin here. In that same instant of your death, you are given the opportunity to see why people did things to you that were harmful or unjust. You finally see the "why" in someone's actions. You can see the reality they were coming from, which is their own belief system. My mother was really trying to protect my daughter. In her heart, she did what she thought was right and good. And how could I not forgive her instantly knowing why she did what she did? Of course! There was nothing to forgive! She was loving me and my child! I bless her for all her love even if it was displayed in a less than perfect way! We are humans!

So when you cross over, you see all the reasons why things happened to you. Why your mother didn't love you enough, why you didn't get that job you wanted so much, everything. And in that instant you see and finally understand and forgive those that have hurt you in any way. "Father, forgive them for they know not what they do." You suddenly know what you have done and why others did what they did to you. Without a doubt, it was a life-changing experience for me. It taught me that I will be the judge of myself.

It is in this review of your life, seeing what you have done to others and what others have done to you, that you both give and receive forgiveness to and from everyone and everything in your life. Of course, you can refuse to give and receive forgiveness. In this case, since forgiveness is your choice yet you refuse to forgive, you can choose to stay in the Lower Worlds until you change your mind. Some souls stay there until the one they can't forgive also crosses over in death. This person has this same experience at their moment of death, of seeing what really occurred with you at that time during their life. Then, and only then, when the first soul is sure that the one he couldn't forgive sees what really happened, can and does he finally forgive him. Then they both can go into At-One-Ment. It is not God who decides this. It is your free-will choice. Creator wants unity. Creator has always offered you complete Union in Creator, with Creator and through Creator. For this I get on my knees and give thanks!

I chose to come back to this world and complete my life here. It was my choice to either stay or come back to this life. I did so because my little girl was only 3 years old and I was a single mom. As much as I wanted to go to that At-One-Ment, I also knew that Source had given me a gift here and a responsibility to this little girl who I loved so dearly as well as to all of you reading this book, so I came back.

It is not Creator who will forgive you for what you believe. Creator is beyond forgiveness as Creator can see exactly why you believe what you believe and exactly why you have acted, thought and spoken as you have. Creator does not judge. Creator is complete and total Love. It is you who will judge you. It is you who will see that because of a wrong belief, you forced your employees to wear red ties. It will be up to you to forgive yourself for that and to ask their forgiveness for making them do that.

In the end, what I have learned most is to not judge others. When I looked upon my life, I saw that the most grievous errors I had made were in judging others. As I judged them, so did they judge me. These were the hardest things to obtain forgiveness for. I created wrong beliefs for them and then they continued to live with wrong beliefs because of me. This is the worst feeling one can experience.

So I do not judge. My Creator, help me not to judge, because I don't want to make that most grievous error.

If I do not judge others, I also don't need to judge myself. Sure, I can see my errors and correct them, but that is not judgment. That is being human and taking responsibility for my life.

But if I judge, I am judged, and that is the worst conclusion. So it is up to me to examine my beliefs and to try to maintain good and true ones. This is what Buddhism is all about. This is the purpose of 'recapitulation' in Shamanism. We have many tools available to us to help us with our beliefs. And basically if you do no harm to yourself or others, if you are living a life free of judgment with a decent belief system that you monitor, and you are impeccable in your thoughts, words and actions, you are preparing yourself for complete union in Spirit. In so doing, you will find that union within this life here and now. Yes, you do not need to wait until you die to achieve unity with Source. It is here and now! Jesus, Buddha, Moses, Mohammed, Krishna showed us that it is possible for a human being to be in complete unity with Creator on this planet, now. Reach out for it, as it is here and available to you right now. We are all human! Creator knows that! Creator isn't waiting for you to become something else! Creator isn't waiting at all. You are waiting. What are you waiting for?

31. "You frequently use the terms Causal and Buddhic. What are their meanings?"

We have seven bodies in our being: physical, mental, emotional, Astral, Causal, Buddhic and Atmic. When you reach your Atmic self, you no longer are incarnated into this physical world. Metatron, Jesus, Buddha, and Djwahl Khul for examples, have "ascended" to their Atmic selves.

Everyday people live from their first three bodies, physical, emotional and mental. But easily accessible with your everyday consciousness is the Causal plane. It is slightly above and apart from your lower 3 bodies. It encompasses them and yet steps a bit farther up where you can see those bodies and observe them. The Causal state is a place of observing from your Causal self. Better decisions can be made here, forgiveness comes easily here, and your sense of purpose is evident here. It is a great place from which to live a more authentic life. It takes practice to keep walking your path in your daily life from your Causal self, but it is worth it in terms of joy, compassion, and fulfillment.

When you are focused on your physical self, like an athlete who is running a race, it is your dominant self. In this state, you are not thinking or experiencing emotions very much at all. You are concentrating all your energy into your physical body to run the race. It would not be a good time to take a math examination.

When you are focused on your emotional body and it is dominant, you are feeling things intensely, but your physical body would not, since it isn't dominant, be able to withstand running a marathon and your mental body would not be able to do well on a math test because you are focusing all your energy on your emotional body.

When you are trying to do computations or math homework, you are dominant in your mental body. So you are not able to experience emotions strongly or use your physical body to run a marathon at the same time, either. In short, only one body is able to be dominant at any one time so balance is what is required.

You need to balance these four bodies to enter the Causal self. Now if you are in your Causal body, you are standing over and above these other bodies and from here you are able to observe your others bodies and watch them work.

The balanced Causal state is a place of non-judgment and non-thinking, solely a place of observation from above your physical, mental or emotional self. It is often found through meditation, that clear place where thoughts are few and unimportant; from a centered place. From this place you can see what is really going on with your lower bodies and you will often laugh at yourself for getting upset or frustrated, as you can now see what little it matters.

Let me help you get to this place of experiencing your Causal self. Try this visualization. This is not a journey; it is only a visualization. Find yourself a quiet place where you won't be disturbed and center yourself, relaxing your body and mind. Then imagine that over and above your head is a control booth. This is the control booth that the director sits in when she films a TV show. It has all the camera screens and volume controls, and it looks down on the stage where the actors are taking her directions and playing out the scene. She can stop the action anytime, tell the actors to perform in a different way, choose which cameras to use and decide which tools and controls, of all those available for her use, she will employ. So you imagine a control booth above your head that looks down on the stage of your life, where you are the actor. You can see the stage over there in the distance, and you can see this control booth just above your head. Enter the control booth and sit down in the director's chair. Take a look around the control booth and find all the switches for play, rewind, fast-forward, stop, and volume.

Now look out the glass window towards the stage and see yourself as if you were replaying a scene from your past. Just watch the action from the control booth. You are not down on the stage; you are in the control booth watching yourself having this experience. You can see the emotions you had at that time but you are not feeling them in the control booth. Just watch the scene and yell "Cut!" whenever you wish.

This is the place of the Causal self. This is the place of observation from a distance. Now what happened on that stage that you would like to change? Imagine that you are telling the actors on the stage to perform the scene differently. This time, cause something else to happen, something that you would rather have had happen, and imagine saying "Action!" to the actors. Again, observe the scene without emotion and without analyzing it. Just observe. Yell "Cut!" whenever you wish. Notice what the actors say differently and what emotions are felt differently. What physical actions were different?

From your Causal self, you have control over your physical self, your emotional self and your mental self. This is a very important body to learn about as it is your higher self, your knowing self, the self that makes the best choices. From the control booth you can tell yourself to feel happier, not to worry about things, and even to avoid making a wrong choice.

Now while you are in your control booth, you see a window that looks outside the building. Look out that window. What do you see outside? Tell me in an email what you see out this window.

I hope you will do the work to get to know your Causal body. When a Shaman walks with one foot in this world and one foot in the next, he is walking with one foot in the physical and one foot in the causal. It is good to learn how to do this.

Act out a scene in which you experienced a belief that does not work for you anymore. Then change the belief to something that does work and play it out again.

When you are walking daily in your Causal self, you can find yourself reaching even higher in your bodies up to your Buddhic self. Most humans never reach this place in their lifetime. It is the place of the Bodhisattva; the one who does not need to return for another lifetime but chooses to do so out of the desire to help other people "ascend" into their higher selves.

I had someone ask me why children who are tortured and killed. I believe those children are Buddhic beings who come here specifically for that purpose-to teach others. In the process of this killing, we humans are having our consciousness raised to be aware of injustice and are given an opportunity to work within our human system to end suffering. If we never saw anyone suffer, we would never do anything about it. So they are clarions, martyrs by choice, to wake us up to our responsibilities to our human family. If we go through this life and never do anything to bring peace to our planet, we have really missed the boat!

To reiterate, the Buddhic state is a state of being above the Causal that you can reach for in this lifetime. You have to achieve the Causal state first. It is a process, but it is possible. Someone asked me how to reach the Atmic state. I answered with a huge smile on my face, "Let me know when you reach the Buddhic state and I will discuss it with you from there!"

32. "Is there a parallel between Buddhism and Shamanism?"

A wonderful book that I love is *The 37 Practices of Bodhisattvas* by Geshe Sonam Rinchen. This book shows us the Mahayana path to perfection. It explains what a Shaman is. A Shaman is a Bodhisattva when practicing the art of healing impeccably. Here are some excerpts of importance:

> "The closer we feel to living beings, the more we wish to help them overcome their suffering, which seems unbearable. This impels us to accept personal responsibility to rid them of it and bring them happiness. We then make the commitment to achieve enlightenment in order to carry out our resolve."

This is the practice of achieving impeccability for a Shaman. Continuing on:

> "Having aroused a strong feeling of compassion, wanting to free them from suffering, we start with those in the hot hells, taking on the anguish caused by heat and fire. It leaves through their right nostrils and comes towards us as a black ray which enters our left nostril. It doesn't just

> vanish into our body or elsewhere but strikes and decimates the selfishness massed at our heart...
>
> Similarly we take away the suffering of those in the cold hells, of hungry ghosts, animals and all the different forms of human suffering of which the principal are birth, aging, sickness and death. We take on the suffering of the demi-gods, who constantly experience jealousy, and of other celestial beings, who feel distraught when they approach death and realize that they must take a less fortunate rebirth."

Here Geshe Sonam Rinchen is speaking of Shamanic worlds and the beings encountered there, along with ways to work within these worlds. Interesting how Shamanism correlates so completely with Buddhism! This is what I was searching for as I studied with my friends and teachers from Tibet.

He continues, "Giving begins with a stream of white light which leaves our right nostril. For those in the hot hells, for instance, our body turns into rain which extinguishes the blazing fires and brings coolness." And further he says,

> "When we are familiar with the practice we take on the suffering as we breathe in and give happiness as we breathe out. One day, we may actually become able to do so. This is a very potent practice, and since mind and breath are closely connected, doing it will increase our love and compassion."

These are also the qualities of a teacher-compassion, impeccability and taking personal responsibility for what is taught. I take these personally regarding my teaching of Reiki and Shamanism. For the longest time I did not think my teaching was sufficient, so I did not teach. But as I was seeing Shamanism dying around me, I was given a dispensation to teach all who would hear. Therefore, my courses are online and ongoing to reach as many as I can before I go on to other worlds.

What kind of spiritual teacher should we seek? The Mahayana Buddhist teachers tell us that:

> "...a peacock-like spiritual teacher is best. Peacocks look rather plain and lumpy from a distance, but when we get close we discover the iridescent beauty of their glorious feathers... an affinity between our own and our teacher's disposition and interests is important... a spiritual teacher should not only possess a good knowledge of what must be cultivated and discarded but be able to explain it correctly... he or she should be compassionate and motivated by a genuine wish to help... trust and confidence are vital... knowledge, kindness and good ethics are essential."

And what qualities must a student possess? Geshe Sonam Rinchen tells us,

> "...the most important are open-mindedness, intelligence and enthusiastic interest...a student must have faith, respect and a willingness to please the spiritual teacher through his or her actions."

And the five faults

> "laziness, forgetting the focal object of meditation, agitation and slackness of concentration, not applying antidotes to these faults when necessary and applying them when it is unnecessary."

One last quote from Geshe Sonam Rinchen's book describes the five kinds of good fortune,

> "That a Buddha has come to the world; that he has lit the lamp of the teachings; that these teachings are alive insofar as there are people who hear, think about and meditate upon them; that there are those who can be looked upon as role models because of their exemplary practice of the teaching; and that support and encouragement for practitioners is available."

In this manner, I must strive to be an impeccable student, a Bodhisattva for those who come to learn this way to At-One-Ment and healing through Shamanism.

My years of study with Tibetan Lamas have taught me the connection between all healing practices. Rather than condemn one method and embrace another, we can see the universality of them all. Healing is healing. If a system heals, then it is worth studying and practicing. No one method seems right for all. That is why I have studied so many methods in my life, so that I could appreciate them all, understand the practitioner of each and respect and honor that practitioner whether he is a Catholic priest or a Haitian Witchdoctor. It has been a hard life for me personally, but a rich one, full of wonder and mystery and an intimate connection to the Source of Oneness beyond imagination!

33. "How does the Shaman define soul and spirit?

"Is this different in terms of religious definitions? Some say the soul is the external intelligence ……the essence of our being…and the spirit is the vibrant energy of the soul, i.e. the prana or chi! Would you clarify this for me?"

Allow me to preface my answer with this fact, that I can only tell you my own views on soul versus spirit. I cannot speak for all Shamans, all people or actually anyone else, except me. I hope you understand. And I don't deny what others say, either. We each have our own reality and it is as we created it. What we believe forms this reality. As we've discussed before, a lot of our beliefs come from our parents, relatives, schools and churches, and unfortunately a lot of it may not be helpful to us. And do we ever take the time to go back and look at what we believe? If we could take the time to re-examine our beliefs, to throw out what doesn't work and adopt what does work for us, we would all be better off. And I hope my course leads those who are ready to do just this.

In my belief system, the Spirit is the One great Universal Oneness, the At-One-Ment, the Source of which we are all part. We all are part of Spirit, so we have this Spirit inside us and around us. We are completely made of this Spirit, "God", if you will. I prefer "Creator" for mine is a loving Creator capable of no less.

The soul, in my belief system, is our spiritual nature, our Atmic self that we always have and carry from lifetime to lifetime. It is this Atmic soul that we are trying to raise to the Logoic plane and eventually to At-One-Ment or complete infusion into Spirit or God.

So the soul is not really a thing but more like a measure of our level of separation from Creator. It is that part of us for which we need to gain the grace, the gong, the quality necessary to complete ourselves in total union with Spirit. It has been attained by humans. We have some Ascended Masters, some Bodhisattvas… amazing humans such as Jesus and Buddha who have completed this union. So it is not impossible.

I feel our mission here is to gain grace or gong. You are familiar with Chi Gong. Chi is energy, the cosmic energy force. And Gong is the practice of obtaining this energy force. So I call it "Grace by Gong" as we are here to practice the obtaining of grace through the practice of being the best we can be as human beings and being in service to those around us. Is Chi grace? Chi has gotten a bad name for itself. We know it is energy and we desire energy, but it's generally seen as purposeless. "OK, so now that I have a lot of chi, what can I do with it?", you may ask. Grace, on the other hand, has a purpose. It is that quality, substance even, that lifts us ever closer to complete union with Spirit. If you can see the purpose of Chi as being the same as grace, as I do, then call it Chi. If grace is a nasty word due to your upbringing, then choose another. It is only language, and language cannot adequately express what I am talking about.

So what separates us from Spirit? Only ourselves. We make the choice. We make the intentions in our lives, and we either act or do not act on them. We create our realities so that what we believe is what we get. We either choose to increase our Gong and end the separation from Spirit, or we don't.

I believe in One Source of Universal Light and Love. We are all part of that Source, Spirit. We all have Spirit. The degree to which we choose to separate ourselves from that Spirit is up to us. And the measure of that separation is the state of our soul.

34. "What good are emotions?"

The power of emotion is a subject that few have talked about, yet it is a gift given to us of immense value. A Shaman not only realizes the value of emotion but learns to control that power to effect healing and manifestation of all good things. After all, healing is a manifestation of health. The hunter in the forest waits for his prey patiently and with emotional control. He does not shout out when he sees a deer or moan loudly when the day is rainy. He controls his emotions to manifest food for the tribe.

But what is the power of emotion? Have you ever been to a football game and really gotten into it, cheering and clapping, and when the game was over you were surprised to see how fast that time flew by? Perhaps you felt this when you went to see a fantastic movie. Or have you ever sat in the dentist's chair for 20 minutes and felt that it took forever? It was your emotions that caused time to speed up or slow down. When you are excited and happy and really into something, time has a way of speeding up and the event passes quickly. But in the dentist's office, you may have felt worried and frustrated, not wanting to be there, so time took forever. So positive emotions speed up time and negative emotions can slow time down. This is only one example of the power of emotions, but I offer it as the first example because we all have experienced this in our own lives.

Shamans, watching and observing emotional power over thousands of years, have honed the manipulation of emotional power down to a science. It is called "time travel" or "time shifting" in Shamanic terms. It is used to create time to prevent an accident, time to allow for necessary things to occur, or time for someone to change one's mind. The power is in the emotion. Controlling the emotions controls the power.

In some cultures when someone dies, the paid mourner ladies come into the house and wail as loudly as they can for days. Funerals are met with sadness and seem to go on for a long time. The survivors do not want to part with their family member and so they extend time with sadness to make the time seem longer before burial. So a Shaman can intend for his own emotions to be sad, forlorn, frustrated, worried, or annoyed, to make time slow down so he or she can get the work done that he or she needs to do.

And what about your own personal emotions? Have you ever thought or realized that you have control over your emotions? Do you know that they are just like the buttons on the soda dispenser machine that can be pressed to choose which flavor of soda you prefer? Do you realize that they are about as useful as a can of cola? Sure they nourish you, but they do so with empty calories while wasting your time and money!

A Shaman will tell you that the only reason for emotions is to manifest what is needed for healing! Don't waste your time feeling jealous, hurt or angry. You will just extend the length of time of the apparent hurt. And if you want to savor a beautiful thing or spend quality time with a loved one, don't get too excited about it or it will be over in a flash.

Many people today run their lives by how they feel emotionally. For every single thing that happens, they judge its goodness by asking themselves, "How does this make me feel?" If you think about it, you may be one of those who can admit that you ask yourself that question as much as one hundred times each day. But is that any way to run your life? Perhaps today, taking a bath makes you feel terrible, so you do not take a bath. But next week, taking a bath will make you feel good, so you take a bath. Running your life on feelings in this way becomes a whimsy, a folly, and a willow in the wind without any rhyme or reason. And yet, this is really how many people judge everything that comes and goes in their lives! How can any decent choices be made like this? Where did we learn this?

We learned to live based on our emotional responses when we were very little. If we wanted something, we yelled and cried and carried on until we got it. We learned that expressing negative emotions would get us what we were looking for from our parents and siblings. We learned to manipulate others with our emotions to get what we thought we wanted. And what we wanted changed all the time. But for many, it has always been, "How does this make me feel? If I feel good then I keep it and get more. If I feel bad then I throw it away, even if it was really good for me or even if I will probably want it tomorrow." We let emotions rule our lives, even though they are nothing but buttons on a soda machine!

Emotions can't gain you success, abundance, happiness, or right relationships...or can they? The Shaman says that by controlling your emotions you gain the power of emotions to manifest healing. And it's true! By eliminating negativity in all its forms in your life, you attract goodness to yourself. Positive attracts more positive. By actively controlling your emotions and seeing that each time you think a negative thought you immediately and consciously replace it with a positive, happy, uplifting thought, you can completely turn your life around from losing to winning. Many of our modern gurus have written books on this subject. Read any one of them- they are saying to control your emotions in order to change your life. A Shamanic truth!

Get the attitude of a winner and start winning!

"The real secret of success is enthusiasm."

—Walter Chrysler

"When we direct our thoughts properly, we can control our emotions..."

— W. Clement Stone

"Take control of your consistent emotions and begin to consciously and deliberately reshape your daily experience of life."

—Tony Robbins

"A man who is swayed by negative emotions may have good enough intentions, may be truthful in word, but he will never find the Truth."

— Gandhi

Be in control of your emotions-don't let them be in control of you. Because if you let emotions run your life you have given up the rudder and sails of your ship and you are floundering around, going nowhere.

It is imperative that a Shaman be in control of his or her emotions. Many forces in the universe know what "feel good babies" we are and come to play on our weaknesses. They tempt us and prick us with things that push our buttons to cause us to rely on our emotional selves. Why do they do this? Because they are not human and do not have the beautiful power of emotions. They are jealous. If they can't play like us, they want to watch us "play" in possibly negative ways. They, too, know the power of emotion and that only some sentient beings have this power. They watch us as we throw it away frivolously instead of taking control and using the power of emotions to manifest joy, healing, abundance and beauty. Can you imagine how silly and soft we look to outsiders?

If you want to heal, think healing thoughts, get excited about healing, work yourself up into a healing mode...really put yourself into it. Shamans use drumming and chanting and power songs and dancing to bring the power of emotions into their healing ceremonies. Remember that football game? Get into your intent for abundance, healing or joy. Sing, dance, and pray out loud.

With the proper intent set in place and the proper degree of emotion as well as the knowledge of the ways to accomplish it, anything can be yours, including a complete remission from cancer. I have seen this with my own eyes.

> "There are two trees, each yielding its own fruit. One of them is negative... it grows from lack of self-worth and its fruits are fear, anger, envy, bitterness, sorrow—and any other negative emotion. Then there is the tree of positive emotions. Its nutrients include self-forgiveness and a correct self-concept. Its fruits are love, joy, acceptance, self-esteem, faith, peace... and other uplifting emotions."
>
> - Author Unknown

Many philosophers and psychologists have sought to do away with emotion, so that by eliminating all emotion we can be centered in mind and body. A Shaman says embrace the power of your gift of emotion but find the knowledge to use it with wisdom in the deliberate creation of goodness. Don't get rid of anything about you. Learn all your tools and then practice with intention and emotional control.

35. "What does personal power have to do with Shamanism?"

Everything. Who do you give your power to? You give it to a doctor when you go for treatment. You give it to your spouse when you do something for him or her that you would not necessarily do otherwise. You give it to your children when you do things for them that you might not normally do. You give it away when you give in to someone else's wishes, desires or demands; when you allow someone else to control you in any way. When you say, "Feed me, heal me, and support me" in any way emotionally, mentally or physically, you are giving your power away.

Some people find it easier to give their power away than to own their power. It may feel easier to say, "Feed me, heal me, and support me!" than to do it yourself. And so we have codependency and unhappy relationships. The truth is, no one can feed you, heal you or support you in the manner that you can for yourself. Why? Because no one loves you as much as you love yourself. And that is the way it should be. Jesus says that all the commandments boil down to this: "You shall love the Lord your God with all your heart, and with all your soul, and with all your mind." This is the greatest and first commandment. And a second is like it: "You shall love your neighbor as yourself."- (Matthew 22:34-40) You are actually supposed to love yourself at least as much as you love others. But we don't love ourselves very much, do we?! In fact, we love everybody else far more than we love ourselves. And because we don't love ourselves very much, we let other people take over where we should be in control. We feed the needs and desires of other people and put our own on the back burner. And after a while we start to resent those people we are feeding because we are starving and we think that it is their fault. But it is not their fault.

Everyone is out there trying to get the best for themselves. Your kids are looking out for themselves. Your husband/wife is trying to get what he/she needs. Your parents are trying to get what they need. And instead of you trying to get what you need, you are out there giving everybody else what they need, what they ask for, and what they desire. Guess what? They will get what they need whether you are the giver or not. The point here is... who is getting you what *you* want?

Now, if I am completely washed up here and you are one of those people using others to get what you desire, well the same thing applies. Only you can give you what you need. If you need healing, you will find the very best and easiest way to get healing right inside you. If you need love, the greatest and freest love is right inside you. If you need support, you can support yourself. If you need food, you know how to work for it. When you understand that loving yourself and caring for yourself is the only responsibility demanded of you, your life suddenly becomes a joy to live! You are not responsible for Mom, Dad, Grown up Children, Hubby or Wife. You are only responsible for you! It's so much easier! And then you can start to really love yourself, to be kind to yourself, and to care for your needs, your desires, and your wishes. Believe me, no one else can really do it for you. They can try and you can ask but no one can do it like you can.

And don't worry about Hubby/Wife and Grown Up Junior. They will continue to take care of themselves. They may beg or plead with you because you turned off your "easy-access faucet". And they will respond by either turning on their own ever-present Source for themselves, or they will find someone else they can drain, deplete or "leech off". They don't need to "leech off" you. It is not good for them anyway. They need to learn to love themselves, too.

You know, this life is short. I would hate to see you leave without learning that you can love yourself and give yourself everything you need to be happy and absolutely joyous. Wouldn't you like to try it once before you go? Isn't that perhaps the lesson you are here to learn, the thing that you came here to experience? Isn't the lesson to love yourself unconditionally, completely and absolutely, knowing that you are fully capable of caring for yourself in every way with abundance, prosperity and joy? You can start today. Stop fulfilling everyone else's demands and make a list of what you need. Start fulfilling that list. No one else will really do it for you. But you know yourself better than anyone else on this planet. You know what you need and how to give it to yourself. Start today. Are you willing to do this?

And once you have your own happiness, security, and abundance under control, then you can love others as you love yourself.

36. "What do you mean by the word 'intent'?"

There are 3 elements to being a Shaman: intent, emotional control and impeccable skills. Let's look at intent.

> "Intent is not a thought, or an object, or a wish. Intent is what can make a man succeed when his thoughts tell him that he is defeated. It operates in spite of the warrior's indulgence. Intent is what makes him invulnerable. Intent is what sends a Shaman through a wall, through space, to infinity."
>
> – Carlos Castaneda

Intent is the basis of manufacturing anything in this reality, including healing and manifestation. Reality is really like a manifestation machine. It is just that we don't use our will or intent to make it the best it could be. Often we say we want something, but deep down in our hearts we really don't want what we ask for.

> "Science is nothing but developed perception, interpreted intent, common sense rounded out and minutely articulated."
>
> – George Santayana

Our reality is completely and entirely based upon our beliefs. You say, "How can that be? I did not create this world, this country or this house." But you do accept the beliefs given to you by your parents, your relatives, your school, your community, and your society. We have been taught as babies to accept the realities of others for generations. This is simple Sociology 101. We are even taught to fear anything but these realities and because of this belief, life changes at a very slow pace, indeed!

So yes, you aligned your intent for housing to that of your relatives. Your idea of social success is the same intention as your society at large. This is not necessarily a bad thing! But it shows the power of intent. One more example is the phrase we hear "If it is not good for me or meant to be, then God will not give it to me." I think this is probably a good intent to inherit because you intend only good things for yourself this way. If it is not possible for you to only intend positive things all the time in all ways, then I think you will have to accept the responsibility for the negative things that you have intended from time to time, too. Get my drift? You are responsible.

"It is a sign of considerable advance when a man begins to be moved by the will, by his own energy self-determined, instead of being moved by desire, i.e. by a response to an external attraction or repulsion"

Annie Besant, *The Ancient Wisdom.*

So how do we bring more good things into our lives? By intending only good things. Dwell only on good things. Whenever you think a negative thought, immediately replace it with a good intention. Picture abundance in your life. Practice looking for goodness around you. Intent creates your reality...what are you intending for yourself? For others? You know the phrase, "Be careful what you wish for, you might just get it." I guarantee you will get what you really wish for.

First, you must be in touch with your real wishes, not just your fantasies. Your real wishes are the ones with emotional buttons on them. These are the wishes that make you cry or scare you enough to make you cringe, or bring a huge smile across your face just thinking about them. They sometimes are simply mirrors of what other people told you to wish for. If your father intended for you to be a doctor but you didn't want to become one, you may still walk through your life without a purpose because you accepted your father's intent for you all along. Belief counseling may be recommended here.

All healing begins with intent. Unless the patient himself intends to get well, the reality will be his own intent of illness. This knowledge can be very frustrating to the healer who knows that complete healing is just a change of mind away. But intent is a free will choice and no one has the right to usurp another's free will. Many times I have wept bitterly before the campfire for those people who chose to suffer rather than to heal. There is only one reason for the intent to not heal, and that is fear.

Isn't it odd that people fear change more that anything else in life? And yet, that is the one thing that is guaranteed with your passage! I invite you all to embrace change. Embrace each new day, each gray hair, each meal, each encounter, and each tiny adventure of every day. Learn to enjoy the most natural thing in life – change. And learn to use it to your advantage.

6   Standing in Your Power

37. "How would you say one develops personal power? I tend to have a very aggressive, controlling personality, which hinders me in many areas."

I think I have tried to answer this question many times, in many ways. Personal power is what this is all about. I am sick over people who hide their heads in the sand and let others completely determine their fates. It is a victimizing world we live in. Many are hungry for power; instead of looking within to the real source of power, some people look at the power of others and try to usurp it for themselves. Some think it is easier to steal than to cultivate. But I disagree. If everyone went within and found their own power, no one would need to usurp anyone else's power and the world would be the gentle, loving place it is meant to be. But unfortunately, our world has always had lazy people, power stealers who are really so weak in themselves. You can learn to take charge of your own personal power. You are the most powerful vortex in the universe! The power is already there within you! You just need to learn how to work with it!

I think the path to achieving control of your power is in:

Knowledge: If you don't know your power is there within you, how will you find it?

Intent: If you don't want this power, you won't have it.

Emotional control: Use your emotions as the tools they are and stop wasting your energy on the "feeling" rollercoaster.

Impeccability: Be the best hunter and warrior that you can be every day. This will bring your personal power to the truest level of Bodhisattva, a true healer on this planet.

You will have many lessons where control is taken out of your hands. You may have had a bunch of them already. There is a difference between control and power. Having personal power is having the security and freedom to let things happen around you in their own way without concern for their outcome. When you go to the ocean, the tide may come in and then go out. You have no concern for the tide. You just observe the tide coming and going and think, "Hey, that's pretty neat!" and you are okay with it happening on its own. You are at peace with it, happy, interested in it, maybe thinking about the scientific causes of it, aware of it, but emotionally stable within your own power. You know you are OK.

When you are assured and comfortable in yourself, owning your personal power, it is an inside thing. You can watch the comings and goings of the day just like the tide. Things can come into your life and things happen and your response is to watch with interest and think, "Hey, that's pretty neat! What a colorful life!" You can let life happen to you and around you without concern or emotional involvement. You know that you are OK. That is part of realizing your mortality. To see that it doesn't really matter what tie you wear today or what car you drive or whether something works out just so. In fact, I get engrossed in the adventure of it. I sometimes like to just wait and see what will happen next. There are a lot of things I just let happen now. And you know what? They always work out. Just like the tides. Given a little time and some general loving feelings that I offer in my prayers to all sentient beings, everything works out in the end.

I don't want my life to be the same each day. If I only have this day, let's see what it will bring. I don't have to be in control of it. If I am in control of it, I am immediately setting up my "How does this make me feel?" boundaries and preventing some neat things from happening. I can tell you that the neat things only come when I have no expectations, no conditions, and no controlling regulations. Living this way, your life becomes much more colorful and you feel like you are really living on the high seas! Don't worry; you can't drown. And even if you did drown, you would not be destroyed. Remember that your spirit is eternal. Death is just another doorway. This world is just another chapter in your book. Go sailing!

38. "I feel I am here to help heal the rifts in Mother Earth's energies. Can you tell me how to go about this?"

There are many power spots on the face of the earth, some good and some not good. When I went to the four corners of the United States: Arizona, New Mexico, Colorado, and Utah, I encountered a place considered holy by the indigenous people there. They said it was the place where souls are born and come from and where souls go into when they die. It is called a place of emersion. I was driving along the area where the Great Sand Dunes National Monument is located and I felt a huge curtain of energy. I am very familiar with vortices but this was different. It was like a huge drapery curtain. On one side was a vortex spinning clockwise like a tornado that covered the whole area. Right next to it on the plains side was another huge tornado of energy spinning counter clockwise. They were fighting each other and between them was a hole, a portal, a gap, a curtain and this gap was not good for the earth and its people. I felt the negativity there and it made me sad and kind of angry as though we are being threatened by it. I didn't like being there as I could sense this rift between two seeming universes. It felt like a place where other beings from other universes could easily access us through this crack in the earth's energy. While at Great Sand Dunes I did ceremony with others to try to close this gap. Many prayers and good energy were offered by my fellow healers and some even tried to energetically sew the ripped seam together again. I don't know if any of this did any good. It seemed too big to fix and had been there longer than humans have existed.

As I drove back to Albuquerque I noticed that on the plains side of this energetic curtain is the largest concentration of alien sightings in America. All the UFO stuff is there, the government buildings where they supposedly caught UFO aliens in the 50s, even tourist locales for sighting UFOs! I was stunned!

Yes, there are places where energies are rifted. And some of us are called to heal these places. This one I am speaking about is being worked on by many healers all the time and yet it is still there. When someone else's reality creates something, it is hard for someone else to uncreate it. Realities like these must be uncreated by the ones who created it. That would be the easiest way. But what can we do to stop these negative influences on our planet? Some sources tell me that there will always be good energies and bad energies on this planet. It is part of the collective consciousness, and we are all under the influence of the collective consciousness to some degree. This one is particularly difficult because of its size and age. It is part of the collective consciousness of a whole society from another universe, perhaps a whole planet of beings from somewhere else, or even from many planets or places. And because it is very old, it is very ingrained in their minds. It would be like trying to remove the Bible from planet Earth in one swoop. It is such a strong belief. This rift on our planet is obviously beneficial to some group, so they protect it just as our collective consciousness would protect the Bible.

But I believe that there are healers incarnating today for the purpose of closing these rifts. I know there are organizations whose purpose is to close rifts on our planet. They may call themselves funny names and seem to have weird ideas, but they exist nevertheless.

One organization involved in Ascension has been working with the energies at Mount Shasta for a long time. They feel that Mount Shasta is a place where ascended beings can come into and out of our universe via a special vortex located there. But they work to keep Mount Shasta a positive place of power and light. They protect this portal and welcome in those beings who may come here to help us. Sedona is another example of a power place. And many people have gathered there to live and to protect that place in its peace and light. I found four vortices in California, and while I was there I protected those places of power myself.

So what to do? It is difficult, as I say, to change the mindset around a power place, be it a positive power place or a negative power place. Protecting a positive place is easy. You just bring your power and light like water for the flowers and offer your light to meld with the good light there. By adding your stick to the fire, the fire glows more brightly. It is healing both for you and for the power place. But you can get caught in these negative energy rifts. They can take you up or down depending on what current you get caught in. It is truly like two tornados side by side going in opposite directions. You may easily get caught in one or the other. It is nearly impossible to stand between them. The friction is too great to stand still.

I would research these power spots and learn about them. I would read everything people have written about them and then pick a few positive power spots to visit yourself. Learn what you can do to boost a positive power spot. Experience is the best teacher. Ask your guides and elders if you have work to do for them in these places and follow their advice.

Perhaps you are one who is here to help heal these places. I would like to see these gaps closed, the earth healed, and positive energy allowed to enfold Mother Earth completely. Start with the small power spots.

There are different ways to close a small negative vortex. One is to infuse it with positive energy. When an object is spinning counterclockwise (don't get involved in the directions of these power spots; positive and negative both spin clockwise and counterclockwise so you can't define them by that) how do you make it spin clockwise? By reversing the trajectory. How do you make something stop spinning that you cannot touch? By applying equal pressure from the opposite direction. And where do you get the energy to apply equal pressure from the opposite direction? Not from you! Do you want to wear yourself out quickly? Everything is energy and each energy has its own signature. Every atom and molecule has its own energy signature. By choosing the correct energy signature from all the energy that is, and applying that correct kind of energy, the Shaman can balance anything. Which is the correct energy to apply to a negative power spot? Your guides and elders will show you if you are working with them and they feel it is for you to do.

As far as your own personal research, here is an idea for you to become aware of energies. Go down to your local cemetery and just walk around. Try to sense the energies in the ground as you walk by each grave and see what you feel. When I walk in a cemetery I not only feel positive and negative energies, I actually meet many of the people who were buried there. I can see their faces and see their lives. This is just a baby exercise in feeling energies. But it is a start. Then go to a park or forest and lean on an old tree there. Pick up on the energies from the tree. You may sense, as I do, all the things the tree has seen in its several hundred years of existence. I see Civil War battles and fires and floods and all the things the tree has seen. I do this by allowing my positive energy to meld with the tree in a particular way while I keep one foot grounded in its roots and the other foot in my causal self.

This is not everyone's work as not everyone can correctly identify and work with these energies. But, as I said, I believe there are some people who came into this world to work with these energies. They are kind-hearted and compassionate, warriors who are here to heal the earth. Those who are chosen have a special connection, a school of sorts, a teacher for this work. You can ask for your teacher if you feel drawn to this work.

39. "How do I manage my time and balance myself in this hectic world?"

I learned about time management from another great spiritual healer, Joshua David Stone. He has written over 18 books, keeps innumerable appointments, manages a healing facility and, along with his wife, counsels and teaches. He is an expert on Ascension and has found that as he has increased his light quotient, he needs less food and less sleep. I think he lives now on 3 or 4 hours of sleep a day without burning out. My point is that there is a light quotient, a filling of our spirits with Universal Light that feeds our minds and bodies.

We are programmed to think that the only method to regenerate ourselves is with food and sleep, physical things, but there are other forms of food in the universe. How silly of us to think that there would only exist this one physical way in which to regenerate, grow and become healthy! This universe is so huge and there are so many realities out there, that we should place no limitations on any part of our existence! So Creator can give you energy, health, rest and joy if you live in Creator's Kingdom... and we all do!

One teaching about energy comes from the practice called Tensegrity, which is based on Carlos Castaneda's work. This practice consists of a series of specific movements to physically regain and gather energy to use for everyday things such as work and activities. You can find the DVD and more information on-line if you do a search for Tensgrity Exercise DVDs. I have been doing these exercises for years now and I love them. They make my mind grow. They help me gather chi or etheric energy as does the exercise about grounding and protection in Chapter 4.

Another teaching about energy is Falun Dafa. If you don't like the western method of Tensegrity, you can choose to practice this Eastern method of energy flow. It is similar but not identical to Chi Gong. Here again, the teaching focuses on energy conservation and growth. While practicing Falun Dafa, I was able to receive an etheric energy wheel in my third chakra. When it spins outward, I give energy. When it spins inward, I receive energy. It knows in which direction to spin so that I am receiving energy when I am not giving energy. When I rest, eat or take a walk, I am receiving energy automatically. Joshua David Stone also used this technique, although he was not necessarily aware of or practicing "Falun Dafa" per se. These energy practices contain transcendental truths, which are present in many disciplines of different names. Of course, this is just my own experience with these methods but these are some ideas for you to explore.

The Shaman lives in the balance of giving and receiving energy. That is why most Shamans look many years younger than they actually are. We do not lose our life force by depleting it. We take time to receive as well as to give.

If you intend to receive energy for growth, balance, support and strength, you will. I have taught you that intent with knowledge and the correct emotional stance can bring you whatever you truly want. I guess I am living proof of this.

40. "Why do all these difficult experiences keep happening to me?"

We gather tools as we walk the road of life. Many of them we just put away and allow dust to gather on, as though they are bits of intellectual knowledge that have no bearing on our reality here and now. But the Shaman recognizes that every piece of knowledge, even every experience has a direct bearing on the path he or she walks today. My tools are out and polished, taken good care of and ready for use at any moment.

When the hunter sits in his tree watching for a big deer to walk by as food for his tribe, he doesn't just sit there with his knife. He also has his bow and arrows ready. He has a rope to bring the deer back to the tribe and water ready for his thirst. He knows his tools and has them ready. He incorporates rope, iron, water and wood into his hunt, and into his life. He knows his tools and keeps them sharp and in good working order.

I realize the tools I have gathered and the experiences I have had all help to make me what I am today. I throw nothing away that is of value, and I throw everything away that is not of value. Keeping a clean closet and having my medicine bag with me, I am ready to learn and to teach. I have room for more and for new experiences and tools, and my eyes are open to see these.

As an example, I have been reading about the healing properties of different kinds of cactus. Today as I was walking my dog I walked by a beautiful paddle cactus that had buds and was about to bloom. I blessed this experience and thanked Spirit for showing me this beautiful plant and it's healing. Then I walked about four steps and saw at my feet a piece of this cactus plant lying in the road. It had a little bud as well. So again I thanked Spirit for this gift, found a cup, got some soil from the ground and planted the little paddle in the cup and brought it home to be with me here. Is there a meaning to this? You bet!

There is meaning in everything that happens to us. Yes, each experience has a meaning. I continually speak about experience here because so many of my students are focused on knowledge; looking for knowledge, reading, studying, and searching the web for answers, when the answers for the Shaman are in the experience. I think you are beginning to understand this and I hope you will continue to learn from your dreams and from your daily life. Be the hunter and be aware. Ask Spirit what the meaning is and accept the gifts you are shown; don't just throw them into a closet to catch dust, but learn to work with them to find the meanings and the lessons that they contain for you!

41. "Do I control my emotions or do they control me?"

There is a difference between controlling your emotions and stuffing your emotions. To control your emotions you must first experience your emotions. You have to know what feelings are. What it feels like to be angry, to express it, feel it, taste it, and be it. What it feels like to be frustrated, to feel it, taste it, say it, move with it, and be it. You need to experience joy, sorrow, and all the emotions. That is one of the reasons why we are on this earth plane. Control means refusing to let something anger you in the first place. When you journey and you see something scary, are you going to run away? If you allow yourself to be scared, then yes! But instead of being scared, what if you were brave? What if you could pull up the emotion of adventure and excitement instead of fear? Now that's power! And that is pretty much what you need to be able to do. This is what the Shaman practices at all times.

You see, you make the choice of which emotion to experience; you and only you. How? Usually by asking yourself the most commonly asked question by humanity, "How does this make me feel?" I could say that not smoking makes me feel terrible and I really want to smoke, so then I would decide to smoke. Is this a smart choice? Probably not! I could say that I hate doing dishes so I just won't do them. Is this a good choice? Probably not! I could say that going to school each day makes me feel terrible, so I won't go. Good choice? I don't think so! Not a good way to live, is it? Constantly asking yourself, "How does this make me feel?" So many people live their entire lives and make their most important decisions based upon the answer to this question. So they are living their lives based on emotion! Well, that's a pretty unstable way of living since human emotions flip-flop all around and change from minute to minute. It would be somewhat better to make all our decisions based upon our mental selves, although we would then be ignoring our feelings completely and sometimes our gut knows best what is right. Best of all would be to make our decisions from our Causal selves, which in a sense is, indeed, that gut feeling! Do you see the difference between stuffing your emotions and controlling your emotional self? It is important to understand how to avoid stuffing, obliterating, and hiding our emotions but to experience them all fully, to understand them and their importance, and finally to choose what emotion we will experience and when.

42. "I have the sensation of swimming or flying up to a different point in time.

Is this some sort of Shamanic experience, or am I just dissociating from stress?"

This experience has been happening to more and more people as we move along the spiral of earth changes. It happens because there is a message for you in that place you are swept away to. The best thing to do is to be an explorer and look for what is being shown to you there. If it is a memory from the past, let it replay again, but be the unattached observer. Ask yourself, "What do I see? What dynamics are being played out here? What should have happened in this scene that didn't? What is the message here for me? What lesson did I learn here or did I miss?"

These are astral journeys. They are best navigated when you are not working or busy but rather when you are at home and relaxing, so that you can pay attention to them. So make time in your day to go to these places willingly. Put yourself into a relaxed state and just allow it to happen. As you make a deliberate time in your day for these astral journeys, they will not happen as frequently at inappropriate times.

You see, Spirit will teach you fast now because you need to answer your call and walk your path of purpose. If it is easier to teach you with flashbacks and pictures of the future, then Spirit will do that. Spirit is tugging on your coat saying, "Look! I have something to teach you! Look here!"

Your job is to "get" those "Aha, now I understand!" moments.

Be the explorer. Be the newspaper reporter. Get the facts. Learn the message. You have asked for lessons to aid your growth. You are getting them.

43. "I have a hard time staying focused. Any suggestions?"

Can I suggest a walk in a park or the woods? Go without a time frame and give yourself lots of time to just be alone and be aware of what is around you. Stop and lean on a tree and feel its energy against your back. Look up into its leaves and see the colors vibrating and shimmering. Try to feel the tree. Try to taste the tree with your inner senses. What noise is the tree making? Can you hear it? Can you get a sense of what the tree is feeling like? Is it cold or hot, does it feel like cotton or like silk or like taffy? Does it smell like rain or like tobacco or like honey? What does it smell like beyond its physical smell?

Take a blanket with you and find a dry grassy place upon which to put your blanket. Lie down on the blanket or on the grass directly and feel the ground. Is it cold or warm? Is it moving? Is it making a sound? Is there a difference between the grass and the ground? Who else has walked here over the years? Ask the ground to show you these pictures. What goes on in one blade of grass? Choose a blade of grass and try to feel the life inside it, what is going on in there. Does it make a sound? Does it have another face beyond just the face of grass?

As you walk, notice the birds and animals around you. How are they? Are they offering you love? Do they need your love or friendship? Do they react in any way when you offer them your love? Do they seem to be happy to see you?

Then, before you go, notice the people around you. You have connected with many things in this time alone. Now see the people. What are they doing? Pick one out. Does he or she seem happy? Well? Having a good time? Bothered by something? Is there something that you think that person needs? See each person as being in a bubble, a bubble of their own world, their own reality. What color is that bubble? Is it the same for each person? Is it big or small? Do trees have bubbles too? Do animals? Do you? What color are these bubbles? What do the colors mean?

This is a lesson in awareness, as is lesson 1 of the Shaman Apprenticeship Course that I teach at www.shamanelder.com. Use all your senses, both your physical senses and your inner senses as well. Let me know what you observed!

44. "What does a Shaman know that most people don't?"

There are many things a Shaman comes to know over a lifetime of learning and practice. Many of these things are impossible to explain with language. The same can be said for certain tenets in Taoism, Buddhism and other faiths and philosophies. Even beliefs, such as faith, are difficult to explain.

The Traditional Shaman believes everything is spirit. Every rock, tree, fish, animal, person, ocean, planet and universe is an active energy or spirit. The spirit or energy showing itself as a rock is not necessarily just a rock. Looks can be deceiving. But the quality or level of the spirit is evidenced in its physical form. For example, the energy of a rock is slow and at a low vibrational rate. It takes a long time to act but it vibrates for a long, long time. A butterfly has a higher and faster vibration but acts much more quickly and evolves faster.

There are also non-visible spirits in various forms. More than you can imagine. Shamans spend lifetimes learning to "see" and perform various tasks with these spiritual forms both physical and non-physical. Some of these forms are neutral, some are beneficent and some are predatory. Let's look at the predators.

The only spiritual form that can gain "Gong" or grace (the only thing in my opinion that we take with us from lifetime to lifetime) is the human being. It is through experiencing life in all its fullness that we get the opportunity to amass "Gong" or goodness. This grace or goodness allows us to evolve into spiritual beings of greater light. So there are many entities that would do anything to have the experience you are having here on earth. All they need is for you to invite them to come into you and they can then share your experiences or use your energy and perhaps get your goodness or Gong.

They also have limited abilities and powers and they will peddle these to you so that you will invite them into your life. These abilities include the power to attract and repel, the ability of precognition or foretelling the future, as well as limited healing abilities.

A man lost his wife to breast cancer and found himself lost and lonely without her. One day he sent up a wish filled with intent and emotion for a new wife. He didn't care what he had to do to get her or how she would manifest. He would do anything to have a new love in his life. The entities heard this invitation and a new wife did arrive. The entities arrived as well and that man felt as though he had a monkey on his back. He could not explain it and didn't know where the feeling came from. He blamed it on feeling guilty for replacing his first wife. He started going to the local pub to wash the feeling away with alcohol. Of course, the entities loved all this experience and the man eventually became an alcoholic. The man never knew that he intended for all this to happen, and unless he met someone who could remove the entities, he was stuck.

Spirit possession is included in the books of knowledge of almost all religions. In the Catholic and Lutheran churches, exorcism is practiced as a way to remove the possessing spirit.

Soul retrieval is one Shamanic way to heal spirit possession. The Shaman goes to these spirit entities and barters or negotiates the non-manifest entity to leave the afflicted person, virtually reclaiming the soul. It is highly dangerous for the Shaman, as the entities, which do not wish to leave, can attack the Shaman, attach to the Shaman and cause mental, physical or emotional harm. It takes an impeccable Shaman who has the knowledge, emotional control and proper intent to do this healing effectively.

Shamans know that there are three parts to you. They are:

<u>Your Self</u> is that physical, mental, and emotional combination of your being that you have known all your life.

<u>Your Master Self</u> is your Higher Self; that part of you connected directly to the Universal Oneness, sometimes speaking to you as a little voice inside your head or the angel on your shoulder.

<u>Your Second Self</u> is on your right side, is just like your physical self but is not attached to your body. This is the self that Shamans use to travel to the Inner Worlds. It just obeys what you put out for it to do. It is that part of you that accomplishes your intentions.

Your emotions come from your physical body. Your intentions come from your Higher Self (hopefully). Spiritual entities can attach to any of the three bodies, so you must gain the knowledge necessary to guard each of them.

45. "How do you protect yourself from predatory spirits?"

With knowledge. Learn their ways and be aware of them and you can maneuver in life successfully. They are not dangerous if you know what they are and how to avoid them.

If you choose to learn Shamanism, learn all you can about the Inner Worlds in which they live. Here is a surefire practice to keep yourself protected at all times. It's called the bubble of protection. Perhaps you already use something like this, if so, great!

Visualize a bubble around your entire self, enclosing your spiritual, mental, emotional and physical bodies. Some people may see this bubble's aura. The Yaqui call it the luminous egg. I see it as an *egg bubble*. Inside this bubble is Creator's Love and Light that is always with you as you are one with Creator. So picture this White Light of Love and peace all filling your egg bubble inside, more than you could ever use and it feels like home and Love from Source Itself. Feels good!

Then on the outside of this egg bubble we will put a Kevlar type material. Kevlar is the strongest woven material in the world. It is woven micro fibers and this Kevlar surface on your egg bubble filters out negative energy and only allows in positive loving energy. So now you have a natural strong filter around your bubble. By imagining it you are intending it and by intending it you make it so. Now all those errant energies out there, when they come zooming towards you, the positive ones will come through the Kevlar into your White Light and add to it and the negative energies, nasty thought forms, pessimistic ideas and so forth will just bounce off the Kevlar surface and continue on their way.

Of course if you create lots of negative energies with your thoughts, words and actions well you had better ask Source to clean out the inside of your egg bubble with that White Light daily. But you will be protected against anything negative out here whizzing by very easily in this way. I just remember my egg bubble and that is all I have to do. If I am going into someplace I know will be negative I just remember my egg bubble and I am good to go! Actually I try to remember it 24/7.

There is no reason for us to be subjected to every single energy out here and there are zillions of them. With this protection you are OK to go to these slightly higher states of consciousness safely and peacefully without fear. These higher places are right inside you anyway. They are not out there somewhere. They are higher parts of who you are!

I would also recommend asking your guides to assist you before doing any kind of higher state of consciousness work. You may not know your guides yet, we will get to it in lesson 2, but they are surely there and listening and willing to help as they love you so much. Maybe you will notice the presence of someone who must love you very much as you sense a feeling of being loved around you! That would be your guide!

I repeat that the best protection, whether you practice Shamanism or not, is knowledge. A Shaman is a warrior, a sorcerer, a mage, and a hunter. He is on his highest alert, fully prepared, moving deliberately with his intention held firmly in the forefront of his mind at all times, ready for anything. He is emotionally centered while simultaneously feeling the excitement of the hunt and the anticipation of a successful outcome.

No one could sneak up on a good hunter. It is he who is doing the stalking. The hunter knows his skills, has practiced a lot, and knows where to look for the game he needs. His senses are ignited and he can smell the breeze and see in low light. He also knows the danger he is in. He knows his prey may turn and kill him at any minute, so to become lazy or inattentive may be lethal. He knows there is no one there to help him and he knows that he himself can do it best, anyway. He would not be a hunter if he wanted someone else to do the work.

You too, are a hunter here on this planet. You chose to come here, to have this experience so that you could gather the one thing that you can take with you when you leave: goodness, Gong, spiritual energy or light quotient. Therefore, you must develop your hunting skills impeccably. You have all the abilities that you need to gather great power here. It is your task to gain knowledge about your skills and how to use them. Skills given to you by other than your own means are just borrowed from leeching entities and are not worth the cost. Entities have nothing to offer you that you don't already have.

A Shaman walks this dimension in pure peace and joy using his or her physical body to communicate and maintain a physical presence with emotional power on this plane. The Shaman uses the Master Self with its constant, small voice of the Higher Self, plus intent, as the sail and rudder of life's ship. And, with the knowledge of the Inner Worlds, the Shaman uses the Second Body Self to work, to create and to destroy, to attract and to repel whatever the Shaman intends for peace, joy and love.

Bibliography

Besant, A. (2000). *The ancient wisdom: An outline of theosophical teachings*. Kila, MT: Kessinger Pub.

Castaneda, C.. *Wikipedia*. Last Updated 2009. http://en.wikipedia.org/wiki/Carlos_Castaneda

Castaneda, C., & Terra Entertainment (Firm). (2004). *Carlos Castaneda's Tensegrity: Volumes 1, 2 & 3*. Los Angeles, CA: Terra Entertainment.

Castaneda, C., Cleargreen, Inc., & Terra Entertainment (Firm). (2001). *Carlos Castaneda's magical passes: Unbending intent*. United States: Cleargreen. www.castaneda.com

Falun Dafa Association (Sydney, N.S.W.). (2001). *Falun Dafa*. Sydney: Falun Dafa Association.

Makoto Ryu Karate-Do Association. (2009). The Seven Virtues of the Bushido Warrior. Last Updated May 2009. www.gdma.com.au

Rgyal-sras, T. B., & Sonam, R. (1997). *The thirty seven practices of Bodhisattvas: An oral teaching*. Ithaca, N.Y: Snow Lion Publications.

Stone, J.D. *Integrated Ascended Masters University*. Last Updated 2009. http://www.iamuniversity.org/

Thubten, C., & Rgyal-sras, T. B. (2009). *The thirty-seven practices of Bodhisattvas*. Singapore: Kong Meng Sun Phor Kark See Monastery.

Wahls, M. (2005). *Testing the spirits the shaman's way: A "how-to" for everyone*. www.shamanelder.com

About The Author

Shaman Elder Maggie Wahls is a traditional indigenous Shaman who has been practicing Shamanism for over 50 years. She began her apprenticeship at the knee of her grandmother at the age of three. Her lineage has been handed down from grandmother to granddaughter for over 400 years, tracing its lines back to the country of the Ukraine. Over a ten year period until her grandmother's crossing over, Shaman Maggie learned the traditional ways of working with spirit, energy and matter to create healing. She accomplished her first healing at the age of five and took her first journey at the age of ten. The skills and abilities to do this shamanic healing were given to her in a very loving way. She was taught that love is the key to walking the Shamanic path.

After her grandmother crossed over, she continued to study and practice. She attended college where she became interested in the religions of the world. After college she began a ten year odyssey to discover what, if anything, all the religions of the world shared in common. Traveling and studying in many countries, she found that there was only one common truth in religion and that is the belief in a Higher Power. She came back to the United States and became a minister, trying to teach the path to this Higher Power using Christian theology. She became a counselor and healer, and she always gave her love and services for free.

Frustrated with the lack of spiritual progress that people could find within a religious faith, Shaman Maggie set out once again on an odyssey to study what other Shamans were teaching. Because of her lineage, she was allowed to study and sit at the feet of some of the most powerful Shamans around the world. What she found was that they were all teaching what her grandmother had taught her. They believed in the same truths, no matter what country or culture they were from. These truths are in place universally and throughout time. This knowledge secured the value of Shamanism in her heart and she began to practice Shamanism exclusively, with many miraculous cures for thousands of people.

In 2003, Creator asked Shaman Maggie to create a way to reach all those around the world who feel the call to Shamanism. More people than ever before have some connection to Shamanism either through lineage in this lifetime or through past lives. Creator provided a course to teach online and Shaman Maggie presents that course and offers her guidance to hundreds of students each year around the world from the comfort of their own homes. She counsels thousands of people to find their healing, their joy, their balance and awareness through her online, ongoing course. No one has to become a Shaman to take her course. It is universal in scope and teaches solid techniques that anyone can use to stand fully in their power and be free.

Shaman Elder Maggie has been counseling for free for almost 30 years. She has a Doctorate of Divinity and is a Usui Reiki Master Teacher. She is an artist, a mystic, a visionary, a teacher, a friend to all and a lover of life. She is one of America's most beloved teachers of traditional Shamanism. She lives with her two beloved canine friends on sacred, healing land called Life Healing Community, located in the Missouri Ozarks. You can contact her anytime by writing an email to shaman@shamanelder.com. You can also visit her website at www.shamanelder.com. Life Healing Community's website is www.lifehealingcommunity.com.

Shaman Elder Maggie has offered her services both privately and publicly and has traveled the country teaching and healing.

She is a dynamic speaker from the heart who is immediately recognized as very earthy, friendly and full of love.

About the cover

The cover image depicts a "Shaman speaking to lake spirits on Lake Kotan." Photo captured by National Geographic photographers in Western Mongolia. Licensed with permission through Getty Images, Inc.

Index

A
animal totems, 16
Ascended Master, 24, 47
Ascension, 31, 97, 99
Astral body, 13
Atmic self, 73, 81
At-One-Ment, 64, 71, 72, 80, 81

B
Bahos, 39
Besant, A., 90
Bodhisattva, 76, 77, 80, 94
Brujos, 5
Buddhic body, 13, 70, 73
Buddhic self, 12, 76

C
cactus, 101
Castaneda, C., 89, 99, 111
Causal body, 13, 74, 76
Causal self, 12, 74, 75, 76
centering, 49
chakra, 100
  fourth, 35
  third, 50
Chi, 81, 100
control, 94
crystal, 25, 26, 37

D
detours, 18
Divine Consciousness, 20

E
egg bubble, 108

Eliade, M., 3
emotional control, 89
emotional power, 83, 110
emotions, 82–86, 102–3
  control of, 93
energy signatures, 25, 26, 27, 33, 49
etheric energy, 50, 100
etheric plane, 11

F
faces, 28
faith, 8
Falun Dafa, 100
fear, 23, 51–53

G
Gandhi, 14, 85
Gong, 81, 82, 100, 106, 109
gratitude, 13, 14, 15
grounding, 35, 49, 50, 100

H
healing, 19, 24
Hopi, 39

I
impeccability, 89, 94
intent, 89, 93
  and healing, 91

K
Khul, D., 30, 31, 73
knowledge, 93

L
Lamas, 80

lower selves, 13

M

Master Self, 107, 110
medicine bag, 36–38, 101
meditation, 12, 19, 20, 45, 75, 79
mental body, 74
Mount Shasta, 97

N

negative vortex, 98

P

power, 86, 93
power song, 35, 42
prana, 80
Prayer Flags, 39
prayer tree, 39–40
previous lives, 8

R

Reiki, 2, 35, 47, 78
Rinchen, G.S., 77, 78, 79

S

Second Self, 107
soul retrieval, 2, 24, 58, 65

spirit guides, 16, 29, 109
    defined, 27
spirit possession, 106
Stone, J.D., 100

T

talking stick, 46
Tensegrity, 99, 100
The Three Sisters, 38
time, lack of, 3, 18
totem animals, 27, 28, 45
totems. *See* animal totems

U

Universal Oneness, 20, 81, 107

V

visions, 53–55
voices, 29
vortex
    Mt. Shasta, 97
    you, 93

Y

Yaqui, 5, 18, 19, 108